WALPOLE AND THE ROBINOCRACY

Series Editor: Michael Duffy

The other titles in this series are:

THE ENGLISH SATIRICAL PRINT 1600 -1832

Walpole and the Robinocracy

by Paul Langford

CHADWYCK-HEALEY

CAMBRIDGE

© 1986 Chadwyck-Healey Ltd

First published 1986

ISBN 0-85964-175-9

Chadwyck-Healey Ltd
Cambridge Place, Cambridge CB2 1NR England

Chadwyck-Healey Inc.
1021 Prince Street, Alexandria, VA 22314 USA

British Library Cataloguing in Publication Data

Langford, Paul
    Walpole and the Robinocracy.—(The English
    satirical print, 1600–1832)
    1. Walpole, Robert *Earl of Orford*—Iconography
    2. Prints, English   3. Satire, English—History
    and criticism
    I. Title   II. Series
    769′.423   N7628.W3

Library of Congress Cataloging in Publication Data

Langford, Paul
    Walpole and the Robinocracy.

    (The English satirical print, 1600–1832)
    Bibliography: p.
    1. Walpole, Robert, Earl of Orford, 1676–1745—
Cartoons, satire, etc. 2. Great Britain—Politics and
government—1714–1760—Caricatures and cartoons.
3. Statesmen—Great Britain—Caricatures and cartoons.
4. English wit and humor, Pictorial.   I. Title
II. Title: Robinocracy   III. Series
DA501.W2L36 1985   941.07′1′0924   85-6609

Printed by Unwin Brothers Limited, Old Woking, Surrey

CONTENTS

PUBLISHER'S NOTE

In 1978 Chadwyck-Healey published *English Cartoons and Satirical Prints 1320-1832 in the British Museum* in which the 17,000 prints listed in the *Catalogue of Political and Personal Satires* by F. G. Stephens and M. D. George are reproduced on microfilm identified by their catalogue numbers.

British Museum Publications reprinted the Stephens and George catalogue to accompany the microfilm edition and for the first time it became possible for scholars to study the prints that are so exhaustively described in Stephens and George, without needing to visit the Department of Prints and Drawings.

It also made this series possible for it is doubtful whether the seven authors would ever have been able to spend the time in the British Museum necessary to search through this huge collection. As it was they each had access to the microfilm edition which they used for their research.

The reprint of the Stephens and George catalogue is itself now out of print but has been reissued on microfilm by Chadwyck-Healey.

GENERAL EDITOR'S PREFACE

In the course of the seventeenth and eighteenth centuries the English satirical print emerged as a potent vehicle for the expression of political and social opinion. Their development was slow at first, but picking up pace from the 1720s, the prints stood out by the 1780s as the most striking symbol of the freedom of the press in England. Sold usually individually, as works of art as well as of polemic, by the late eighteenth century they constituted the basis of a thriving commercial industry and had established themselves as one of the predominant art forms of the age. The graphic skill of the engraver as well as the pungency of his message makes the English satirical print an immensely attractive, entertaining and very fruitful source for the study of Stuart and Hanoverian England. Surprisingly, although many of the prints survive, this source has been frequently neglected, and it is the aim of this series to remedy that deficiency by showing through the study of selected aspects of the period between 1600 and 1832 how the historian can illuminate the prints and prints can illuminate history. All art forms are the product of particular political and social environments, and this volume together with the rest of the series hopes to set this particular art form – the English satirical print – in its proper historical context by revealing how it gave graphic representation to the ideas, assumptions and environment of that era.

Michael Duffy

PREFACE

The period of Sir Robert Walpole's premiership is well known as one of exceptional importance in political history. It not only saw the personal primacy of Britain's most long-serving Prime Minister, but also marked the establishment of a system of government which broke finally with the instability of the seventeenth century and prepared the way for the development of parliamentary democracy. The period is equally well known for the immense growth of popular and polemical literature associated with the rise of Grub Street. The emergence and establishment of the political cartoon as a native art form is only one, but by no means the least significant, aspect of a great revolution in national culture. The prints reproduced in this volume have been selected with both the significance of Walpole's politics and the significance of the cartoon's development in mind. Such selection is, however, necessarily subject to certain constraints.

First the prints are concentrated heavily in the period after 1733. An effort has been made to include as many as possible from the early part of Walpole's ministerial career, but the chronological imbalance naturally reflects the enormous expansion of publishing in the late 1730s.

Secondly the prints do not faithfully represent the entire history of satirical engraving in the second quarter of the eighteenth century. Walpole's political concerns extended to many aspects of national life, particularly in the 1730s. These are reflected in the diversity of prints represented. But cartoons which were not concerned essentially with the Walpole regime and its manifold consequences are deliberately excluded. This has one particularly important effect in largely omitting Hogarth's prints. To leave out Hogarth may seem akin to staging Hamlet without the Prince of Denmark. But very few of Hogarth's prints in this period were overtly concerned with politics. Moreover his work, particularly the celebrated series of the 1730s, is readily available elsewhere. His somewhat ambivalent importance for the political cartoons is briefly discussed in the Introduction.

All the prints are reproduced from the British Museum collection; the brief descriptions provided are not intended by any means fully to explain the details of the prints, but rather to make their essential purport clear to the reader. A much fuller description will be found in a work which remains a remarkable monument to nineteenth-century scholarship, F. G. Stephens, ed. *Catalogue of prints and drawings in the British Museum, Division 1, Political and personal satires*, vols. II, III.

The prints in this volume are reproduced as far as possible in order of publication. In the *Catalogue* they are placed in sequence according to the date of events depicted in the prints.

Most of the debts incurred in editing this volume are acknowledged in the bibliography; the work of Mrs. George and Professor Atherton has proved as invaluable to me as it will prove to all those who wish to understand the evolution of the political satire. In addition I wish to record my appreciation of Dr. Duffy's supervision as general editor. His kindly but authoritative comments have been of the greatest value.

Paul Langford

INTRODUCTION

I.

The Emergence of the English Political Cartoon

It is a commonplace assumption in the history of English art that the early Hanoverian period saw the coming of age of the graphic print, and in particular of the political cartoon, as a native art form. George Vertue, whose own engraving and publishing activities made an important contribution to this process, was also an engrossed observer and conscientious historian of it. Before the Hanoverian accession, he pointed out, the art of engraving seemed to be regressing. The market was dominated by foreign prints brought in especially from France and the Netherlands. There were few engravers at work in London and most of these were themselves foreigners. At a time, during Queen Anne's reign, of intense social, religious and political conflict a wide-spread and powerful interest in satire was expressed far more readily by literary than graphic means. Thirty years later this situation had been transformed. Vertue picked out 1744 as 'this year or this time the most remarkable for work done or doing in Engraving'.[1] An apparently inexhaustible demand for prints, crude and sophisticated, vulgar and refined, fantastic and historical, solemn and satirical, seemed an established feature of the English scene. In contrast with the tiny groups of artists active in 1713, Vertue was now able to list no fewer than fifty-five copperplate engravers at work in the capital, most of them native Englishmen.[2] Protected, albeit inadequately, by recently enacted copyright legislation, this busy and growing community testified to a veritable revolution in the publishing world.

Vertue could offer no very convincing explanation for this change, though he plainly considered his own art as merely the least developed branch of an under-developed national culture. 'This Nation being not so neare the central warmth of Arts has been slower in the progress and produce of Artists, (of those kinds) than some neighbouring Nations. But of all the branches of Art that of Sculpture Graving has made the slowest advances.'[3] In retrospect it is tempting to emphasise demand rather than supply, and to suggest that an obvious and increasing public need for inexpensive art was bound to provide the necessary stimulus to native genius and energies. What is surprising, however, is that this particular genre lagged behind other developments in the publishing world. The really marked expansion of the literary periodical and topical press had occurred in the two decades following the Revolution of 1688, particularly the first few years of the new century. Possibly this great advance on the part of 'Grub Street' was the natural precursor of matching progress for the engravers and their publishers. But even so there was a perceptible lapse of time between the two, one which is not readily explained in terms of the development of an appropriate purchasing public.

In the absence of obvious alternatives, art historians have emphasised the inspiration of individual artists, and in particular the undoubted genius of one of them, William Hogarth. Certainly Hogarth's character and career provide all the requisite elements.

His originality and independence in the arts of comic painting and engraving placed him head and shoulders above his contemporaries both in Britain and on the continent. A marked, if slightly misleading, insularity of outlook and a well-publicised contempt for the foreign and fashionable qualified him as the natural founder of a truly vernacular tradition. No less important, his dominating, almost authoritarian leadership fostered a succession of artists who, even when they criticised him, recognised his stature and significance in the development of the English school. And finally his shrewd sense of business, which extended even to ruthlessness and sharp practice, made him a most influential, hard-headed figure in a profession not noted for its practical qualities. Among contemporaries and ever since, his life and (if more precision is required) the publication of the first of his great series, the *Harlot's Progress*, in 1734, have constituted a great landmark in the development of English art.[4]

For the art in general Hogarth's importance remains undeniable. For the development of the political cartoon his significance is less certain. Hogarth seems to have had little interest in political satire. At the end of his life he was to engage in a controversial and perhaps injudicious defence of George III and Lord Bute. Apart from this, only in his youth, in the 1720s, did he attempt any significant contributions to the political debate. These prints belong to the period when Hogarth was manifestly bent on experiment, and seeking an independent expression of his talent. They hardly suggest innate enthusiasm for political subjects. His depiction of the South Sea Bubble (3)* hints at the Hogarth of the great series of the 1730s, and reveals more concern with human folly than political satire. The stark symbolism of the uncompleted *Some of the Principal Inhabitants of the Moon* (7) makes no particular political point, and even the scene from *Gulliver's Travels* (8) has more to do with the comic potential of Swift's satire than with its political implications. The temptation for a great artist to join in the controversies of the 1730s must have been considerable, and there is indeed a plausible story that Hogarth was approached by opposition leaders with a commission for a print to be entitled 'The Statesman's Progress' on the lines of the Harlot and Rake. The offer was turned down and the commission subsequently executed in an inferior manner by another artist (42). Hogarth may conceivably have had his own political reasons for declining to become involved in controversy. He had executed a silver engraving for Sir Robert Walpole[5] and seems not to have shared the antipathy of his fellow artists and writers for the Hanoverian regime.[6] He may also have considered it bad for business to take sides. Though the experience of John Gay demonstrated that the financial rewards of opposition could be substantial there were also penalties in alienating the fashionable world of the court. It is difficult to believe, for example, that the copyright act for which Hogarth laboured so hard, would have been obtained as readily as it was in 1735 without the support or at least acquiescence of the government's friends in the Commons. In any event Hogarth's refusal to lend his services to the patriot camp deprived the political cartoonists of a brilliant talent. The wit and savagery which he later unleashed in his notorious study of Wilkes would have found a rich and appropriate subject in the political controversies of the Walpole era.[7]

* Italicised numbers in the text refer to the plates in this volume.

14

II.
Emblem and Caricature

Hogarth would not merely have raised the artistic level of the political satire, had he chosen to engage in it; he would also almost certainly have achieved a major shift in its direction. To some extent he indirectly helped to bring this about anyway. The influence of his great comic series, *A Harlot's Progress, A Rake's Progress* and *Marriage à la Mode*, is evident in the increasingly ambitious political engravings of the late 1730s, particularly in the narrative techniques employed, and the wealth of realistic detail and allusion displayed. It is also more controversially revealed in what is taken to be the central and enduring achievement of eighteenth-century English graphic satire, the evolution of caricature, beyond the conventions imposed by the older Italian and Dutch traditions, into the recognisable art of the modern political satirist. Ironically, no-one would have more resented being given the credit for this development, in one sense at least, than Hogarth himself. For he drew a significant distinction between character as depicted in his own work, and caricature as portrayed by the hacks, especially those engaged in satirising the political world. The distinction was displayed in a didactic print, and worked up into a coherent critical theory.[8] In retrospect his horror at the wilder manifestations of the growing taste for political caricature is particularly interesting. Historians have been understandably concerned to stress the novelty of eighteenth-century art, notably its divergence from the well-established emblematic tradition. However, it is possible to exaggerate the extent and rapidity of the change. The appeal of the emblem long remained a very influential and powerful one, not least in the art of Hogarth and his school.[9] For the political cartoon at least it was particularly important, and showed considerable capacity for survival. Contemporary conditions had a crucial bearing on this. Early eighteenth-century cartoons rarely served the function of their modern counterpart, selecting and satirising a particular issue or personality in an immediate, even ephemeral way. Their relative expense alone[10] made them highly inappropriate as ephemera. Frequently they were designed to serve as a form of narrative, telling a political story which required considerable care and attention in the reading. They could be enormously elaborate and packed with allusion. The *European Race* series (*50, 54, 61*) which displayed in striking detail the intricacies of international relations in the prelude to the War of the Austrian Succession, was comparable in this respect to Hogarth's great narrative works. Such prints were to be read rather than viewed, or even deciphered rather than read. Symbols, emblems, rebuses, the familiar features of heraldic art, formed the natural medium in this process of communication. Contemporaries, used to a setting in which everyday information was customarily conveyed in pictorial, visual form, thought them natural and appropriate.[11] A harmonious confusion of the literary and graphic, so remote from the modern distinction between the printed word and the

15

pictorial image, inevitably had a deep influence on the emerging cartoon. In the most extreme cases it even produced so-called 'hiero-glyphic' prints which in their elaborate but cryptic form rather resemble a modern child's puzzle than a modern cartoon (96).

The emblem remained the natural language of the political cartoon for reasons of expediency as well as tradition. It offered, for instance, some small protection against prosecution. Admittedly, in the reigns of George I and George II there was little effective government machinery left for the exercise of censorship. By continental standards the British press had a remarkable degree of freedom in publishing without advance submission to an organ of the state. But prosecution following publication, particularly for the serious crime of seditious libel, remained a real possibility. This applied as much to the engraving business as to the more conventional letterpress. For example, the Walpole ministry's campaign against Robert Francklin, the printer of the *Craftsman*, involved a print satirising Walpole (see *14*) as well as the better known pamphlets and newspapers.[12] The arrest and detention of ballad and print hawkers, even when they were eventually released without judicial prosecution, were also familiar and irksome tactics of government. In this situation anything which reduced the direct offensiveness of a print, without impairing its impact, was plainly to be valued. Satire, symbol, metaphor, historical analogy and allegory, all had their attractions. At times the results could be bizarre, almost surreal. In the frontispiece to *A Collection of State Flowers* (39) Walpole was even depicted as a gigantic sunflower, in whose shade 'Treasury pinks' and 'Scottish thistles' flourished, while the English rose was uprooted and left to die. The meaning was clear to the most unsophisticated viewer; but with a literal-minded legal profession to deal with, it was not as politically dangerous as might be imagined.

In retrospect Walpole's regime offered stability and security. At the time it was more commonly seen as part of a potentially unstable and insecure situation. The Jacobite threat was much in the thoughts and mouths of the politicians. Plots and counter-plots, many imagined or highly implausible, were a customary feature of political reporting. Walpole's partly genuine, partly calculated fear of the Pretender, and his readiness to use the Jacobite charge to smear his opponents, considerably heightened the resulting tension. In the prints his enemies would be given tartans and the Pretender himself introduced (*101*). Opposition retaliated with improbable pictures of Walpole in a Jacobite kilt, supported by the Pope (*35*). More generally, conspiracy and fear of conspiracy bred a morbid interest in the strange world of the plotter and the spy and added a sinister dimension to the political vocabulary. Codes, cryptograms, symbols, took on additional meaning, and occasionally nature seemed positively to imitate art. Thus, the strange evidence produced against those involved in the Atterbury Plot in 1722 caused great public interest in the hidden significance of an apparently innocuous vocabulary, and furnished Swift with an effective scene in *Gulliver's Travels*. In Lagado Gulliver found a 'set of artists of dexterity sufficient to find out the mysterious Meanings of Words, Syllables, and Letters'. Anagrams and acrostics abounded and absurdly everyday phrases turned out to have important political

16

meanings. A sieve signified a court lady, a lame dog an invader[13] (an obvious reference to the evidence given in the Atterbury Plot), a chamber-pot a committee of grandees. No parody of Swift's could have exceeded the absurdities of reality, nor did the cryptic nature of much graphic satire seem to contemporaries in the least fanciful.

The deep conservatism of contemporary political prejudices may also have helped to preserve the old artistic conventions. More than most periods the 1720s and 1730s were deeply hostile to innovation in politics. The charges against Walpole and the 'Robinocracy' were levelled at what were taken to be deliberate attacks on traditional values, customs and institutions. The *Craftsman* and its allies appealed conscientiously to a well-established 'country' tradition and demanded the restoration or preservation of ancient, historical liberties. It was an ideological position which could readily be expressed in familiar emblems of peculiarly English virtues. Britannia herself was, of course, much the commonest as well as most potent symbol of such virtues. She appears again and again in the prints of the period, lamenting and opposing the corrupt, self-seeking Walpole, exhorting and supporting his opponents, bravely defying every assault on her virtue, defending Magna Carta, the right of merchants, or the royal navy (*31, 35, 46, 57, 61, 80, 87*). Walpole's defenders also sought to exploit so powerful an image (*12*), but like other symbols of nationhood, the lion and the bulldog, she was associated most readily with the patriot cause. The lion generally appeared in sadly reduced condition, thanks to the activities of Walpole. Restrained on a leash (*50*), humiliated by other animals (*61*), deprived of its eyes (*75*) or its teeth and claws (*53*), trailing behind a Spanish plough (*58*), yoked to a barrel of excised liquor (*22*), it represented the potential valour of an England enfeebled by corruption at home and appeasement abroad. Occasionally it could be shown rejoicing at the discomfiture of its enemy, as in the aftermath of the excise crisis when it was depicted complacently, and somewhat comically, smoking a pipe of excise-free tobacco (*31*). The bulldog occurred less frequently but appeared in similar situations. In one print it lies cowed on a French carpet (*61*), in another it is held by a butcher anxious to slip its leash but prevented from doing so by Walpole (*54*), in others it is sullenly inactive (*50, 75*).

These emblems of the true spirit of old England were only a few of the wide range of devices which drew on well-established heraldic or emblematic conventions. Things foreign and things tyrannical offered a particularly extensive choice of symbols. Apart from the fauna and flora – foxes (*50*), cocks (*75*), and fleur de lys (*54*) for France, wolves (*50*) for Spain, boars for Holland (*50*) and bears for Russia (*50*) – there were the inevitable wooden shoes and manacles signifying continental slavery (*5, 22, 26, 36*). Over all presided the great allegorical symbols: Justice with her scales (*26*), Liberty with her cap (*80*), or with broken fetters (*14*), a variety of statuary and heraldry to suggest general states such as trade and prosperity (*26*) or particular qualities such as folly (*2, 9*). Fortune and her wheel were frequently depicted for political purposes and were readily appreciated both by a popular audience which understood the unpredictability of politics and by a better read class brought up to interpret the vocabulary of Machiavelli and Harrington (*59, 101*). Individual figures in the classical pantheon and mythology also made an appearance, especially Minerva for glory (*12*) and the Furies for evils such as envy and sloth (*88*). Less sophisticated, but immensely popular and effective were the dragons and monsters, preferably many-headed, which with the aid of appropriate captions could be made to represent almost any unpleasant practice or policy. Walpolian corruption in general and the excise scheme in particular took on a monstrous form in many prints (*23, 27, 29*) while from the ministerial point of view the very idea of opposition could be similarly depicted (*12*). Such an accessible vocabulary evoked a predictable and potent response from an early eighteenth-century audience. It is not surprising that it was freely used by engravers and artists.

This is not to say that caricature made no inroads on the traditional pattern of graphic satire. The typical print of the pre-Hanoverian period had been an elaborate tableau, almost devoid of personalities or realistic details and dominated by somewhat lifeless allegory. By the early 1740s the elements of modern caricature had unmistakably emerged, with a much more marked interest in individual politicians, and a matching concern with the comic potential of a particular episode or situation. This is perhaps best demonstrated in the prints published shortly before and after Walpole's fall. *The Motion* series of cartoons was a particularly interesting one. Provoked by the failure of the parliamentary opposition to carry a motion demanding Walpole's dismissal, in February 1741, it began with a brilliant attack on the opposition leaders (*82*). Instead of a stylised representation of a typical patriot figure or cause there were careful character studies of individuals ranging from the principal chiefs of opposition, Carteret, Pulteney and Argyll, to less prominent men such as Dodington and Lyttelton. They were shown in or around a coach (representing opposition), which was manifestly running out of control. There were no gods or goddesses, no pictorial emblems or symbols. The result delighted Horace Walpole, who was astonished by the accuracy of the caricaturist and prophesied a golden future for such artists. Subsequent prints in what proved to be the most bitter of all battles of the prints under Walpole varied the metaphor – opposition was given a funeral procession to suggest the death of faction (*86*), while in anti-ministerial prints Walpole was shown making his own progress on a money-chest (*84*), and in a coach from which army commissions were distributed (*83*). In lesser hands than those of the original artist of *The Motion*, the older practices returned. Britannia, for instance, was soon introduced to encourage perseverance by the opposition (*87*). But in retrospect it is clear that *The Motion* and its successors broke out of the established conventions and looked forward to the Darley and Townshend caricatures of the 1750s, even perhaps to the great caricaturists of a later age, Rowlandson, Gillray, and Cruickshank.

Nonetheless the timing of *The Motion* series must be borne in mind, for it came at the very end of the Walpole era. Its most interesting features were largely absent in the years of intense political and polemical conflict between 1730 and 1740, and the most that can be detected during this period is a growing interest in the identification of individual character. An example of this was the readiness of the press, supported by the engraver, to present the debate between court and country as a personal battle between Bolingbroke and Walpole (*16*). Walpole himself obviously gave a considerable stimulus to the emerging fashion for caricature, and the need to bring home to the public an appropriate, recognisable image of him was manifest in many prints (*16, 66, 67, 109*). Yet it is possible to exaggerate the connection of these with the modern conventions of political portraiture. Comparison of the better portraits of Walpole (themselves generally somewhat formal, e.g. *111*), with the prints does not suggest that the satirists were concerned primarily with the reproduction of plausible likenesses. Recognition was achieved not by the selection or exaggeration of facial features, but rather by more mechanical devices: the garter which Walpole took such pride in displaying (*14, 35*), the accompanying impedimenta of office and corruption (*80, 84*), association with his brother Horace (*32, 60*), or simply the use of captions providing clear historical parallels. The latter, comprising Wolsey (*29, 67*), Burleigh (*69*), Gaveston (*70*), Cromwell (*62*), De Witt (*34*), Caesar (*10, 66*) and Sejanus (*34*), performed a double function, making clear that it was the prime minister who was intended, and identifying him with an appropriate villain or hero, as the case may be. His expression was normally shown as coarse, even leering (*53*), but always in a stylised rather than life-like way, and few observers could have been expected to recognise him in terms of verisimilitude. The same impression is gained from the treatment of others portrayed in the prints, for instance George II. Merely to depict the monarch in a semi-realistic, above all critical manner, was itself a major advance on the cartoons of earlier periods. But it did not extend to the presentation of life-like portraits. George II was generally identified by emblems of royalty, such as the crown and sceptre, or by the presence of attendant courtiers (*18, 55*), or by certain well-known personal eccentricities, particularly his notorious habit of kicking his hat. In time this last became the obvious and highly convenient shorthand for referring to him, and doubtless because of its comic potential, gained wide currency (*46, 48, 100*). Identification of this kind, by association rather than recognition, achieved its main object; but it would not have appealed, nor would it have been necessary, half a century later.

III.
Walpole and the Prints

Walpole undoubtedly had much to do with the great popularity of political cartoons in the 1730s but for the first ten years of the Walpole regime there were few cartoons published, and fewer still concerned with politics. This is perhaps surprising in view of the place generally bestowed on the South Sea Bubble and the years 1720–21 in the history of the cartoon. Certainly a great number of prints were put on the market at this time. But the majority originated in Holland and France, and at best were slavishly imitated by English printers. (The interesting prints published by John Bowles and Hogarth's own youthful effort (*1, 2, 3, 4*) were among the very few truly native products.) Nor, of course, did they have much to do with Walpole, important though he was in resolving the crisis, and important though the crisis was in furthering his own career. In the *Brabant Skreen* (*4*), it is probable that Walpole was the politician skulking behind the screen. But even this is far from certain, and the prints generally displayed greater interest in others involved in the scandal: the Duchess of Kendal, the king's mistress, and Robert Knight, the cashier of the South Sea Company, whose flight to Belgium provided enraged and ruined speculators with a suitable scapegoat.

In retrospect the latter part of George I's reign has an obvious importance in Walpole's career and the establishment of the political system associated with him. The skill which he displayed in preserving the Hanoverian dynasty from the damaging effects of the South Sea Bubble was matched by the adroitness with which he exploited the Atterbury Plot and the accompanying political tensions two years later. Unlike the Bubble, the Plot was a matter of relatively small moment and little danger. But Walpole's remorseless pursuit of the plotters and his exaggeration of the threat they represented strengthened him both at court and in the Commons. Hardly less important was his astute management of the Treasury. It could be argued in his favour that he used his authority to beneficial effect in his remodelling of customs duties, his initial care of the sinking fund and his preliminary essays in inland commodity taxation. More important however was the patronage with which the Treasury provided him, and the increasing authority which he displayed in dealing with its subordinate departments, especially the customs and excise. Throughout this process of political and administrative consolidation the engravers and their publishers seem studiously to have avoided politics as a theme as well as Walpole's own growing stature. Only Wood's Halfpence (*6*) was presented in the prints. Even this is best seen as a sequel to the South Sea Bubble, since it seemed to present a similar threat both to sound credit and to political liberty. The agitation was plainly an attempt by Irish opponents of the court to exploit fears of a similar scandal in Dublin. The absence of political prints in general presumably reflects the slow and erratic development of the political cartoon; the absence of comment on Walpole seems less surprising if his position at the time is borne in mind. At court he played second fiddle to his brother-in-law Lord Townshend. In the Commons, by no means the dominant chamber of the 1720s, he was compelled to defend measures which he had had only a small part in making. Foreign policy especially, the most important area of public interest during the European war emergency which existed in the years after 1725, was far from being within his control.

The situation was transformed between 1727 and 1730. Walpole's success in surviving the death of one king and the accession of another, which surprised him as much as anyone, greatly enhanced the general awareness of his importance in the ministry. Any doubt which remained was finally removed three years later when Walpole ousted his brother-in-law in order to give himself a firm control of foreign as well as financial policy. Thereafter the way was open for his emergence as the 'great man', the political prodigy whose ministerial longevity outdid all previous ministers and whose dominance of the parliamentary and political scene was unparalleled. Before 1727 the engravers had not seen fit to include him even in their more political works. By 1742, the year of his downfall, an innocent social satire, such as a portrayal of Vauxhall Gardens, was thought incomplete without him (89).

The special significance of Walpole's emergence as the political colossus of his time lay not merely in his personal primacy but in the way in which it could be associated with some of the deeper and more disturbing trends of the late seventeenth and early eighteenth century. This was to some extent a false association, and was exposed as such after his downfall in 1742. Walpole did not personally create the system of government which he operated in the 1730s so successfully. He had not been primarily responsible for the permanent establishment of mainstream Whiggism in government; this process, achieved by the elimination of the court Tories in 1714–15, the defeat of the Fifteen, the passage of the Septennial Act, and the foreign policy of Stanhope and Sunderland had owed more to his senior colleagues in administration. Moreover Walpole himself had been in opposition for a critical period between 1717 and 1720. Nor could he personally be held responsible for the major trends and developments which ever since the Revolution of 1688 had disturbed critics of government: the enormous growth of the national debt with the corresponding emergence of a monied interest dependent on expanding and expensive government, the establishment and retention even in peacetime of a standing army, the growth of a great patronage machine employed to corrupt both the electorate and the House of Commons. Walpole indeed owed his own success primarily to political tactics rather than grand strategy, and especially to the committed support of the Crown, a commitment which individual ministers had rarely held for prolonged periods under William III and Queen Anne. Moreover, his original contribution to politics – his measures of religious peace, pacific foreign policy, and low, socially regressive taxation, designed to calm the fears of the landed classes – makes him seem even less representative of pre-existing Whig traditions. Contemporaries however tended to see him differently, and it was the way in which he came to stand for an entire system of finance and government which made him so unpopular. Quite suddenly, on the accession of George II, the myriad

22

anxieties and grievances of an entire generation of political malcontents came to be focussed on the career and activities of one statesman. Nothing else could explain the extraordinary effects of country propaganda in these years, nor the way in which generalised critiques of the corruption of early eighteenth-century society and government were instantly translated by an excited public into diatribes against Walpole and his creatures. Neither of the two remarkable works which signalised this process, Swift's *Gulliver's Travels*, and Gay's *Beggar's Opera*, was actually intended by the author as a specific complaint against Walpole's rule. Yet both were instantly interpreted in that way; as the cartoonists were quick to discover, once established, the identification between Walpole's personal primacy and the constitutional ills of England was capable of almost limitless exploitation.

Only slightly less important than this development was a corresponding entrenchment of the forces of opposition on the accession of George II. Before 1727 both discontented Whigs and proscribed Tories had looked to the accession of a new king for a further change in the political pattern. On the basis of experience since 1688, and in the light of the short ministries which had been the rule ever since then, this was a reasonable expectation. Consequently George II's confirmation of the existing ministry and his subsequent narrowing of it with the humiliation of Townshend made additional impact on those disappointed. The result was the emergence of a 'patriot' opposition which was to launch a new, systematic attack on Walpole's ministry outdoing anything since the Hanoverian Accession in force and virulence. It was this opposition, working through the press, which did so much to heighten public awareness of Walpole's position in the years after 1727. The terms Robinarch and Robinocracy emerged clearly at this time, with a wealth of polemical pamphlets, broadsides and ballads, stressing the triumph of the 'robin' first at the expense of the bird kingdom in general, second at the expense even of his friend Tom Tit (*15*). But the patriot opposition did far more than encourage the emerging belief that Walpole as an individual was the enemy of true patriots. It also produced a coherent expression of contemporary political philosophy, and set out to offer a genuine ideological alternative to the existing regime. In doing so it employed a glittering array of literary talent, deeply influenced future generations of politicians, and consciously appealed to a public, extra-parliamentary following. It is primarily in the context of this opposition, that the extraordinary expansion of the market for the political cartoon, highlighted in the great controversies of the years 1733–4 and 1739–43, must be seen. Particularly significant was the strikingly anti-ministerial bias of the great majority of prints. Until *The Motion* series prints in support of government were extremely rare. An exception which proved the rule was perhaps the panegyric published in 1730 (*12*),[14] showing Walpole mounting a triumphal monument, about to receive a ducal coronet from the hand of Minerva. The fact that it was the work of Frenchmen (one of them, Peter Fourdrinier, a distinguished artist in his own right), made it easy for critics to denounce it as the product of Walpole's slavish attitude towards Cardinal Fleury. Moreover, the ducal coronet most injudiciously fed popular suspicion of Walpole's aspirations, and was much satirised thereafter. One or two similar panegyrics appeared during the following years but the market plainly preferred prints hostile to government. Though Walpole went to some pains to influence the press in general, he appears to have made no comparable attempt to have his case put forward in graphic form. The surviving evidence of his relations with the journalists reveals nothing in this way and only one print before *The Motion* series suggests a genuine counter-attack on opposition (71).

The opposition prints are most instructively viewed as part of a co-ordinated propaganda campaign. Pamphlets and tracts developed major arguments in a systematic way for an educated audience. The newspapers served naturally to catch various forms of controversy, ranging from small items of news to the serialisation of substantial contributions to debate, particularly in political weeklies such as the *Craftsman* itself. The ballads and broadsides, hawked about the streets as well as sold by the print shops, concentrated on simplified, popularised versions of the politics of the moment. Cartoons were used in conjunction with all these. Some were actually designed as frontispieces (e.g. 39, 57, 59) and many were issued with a ballad or broadside.[15] One of the poetically more pretentious ballads of the period, Richard Glover's *Admiral Hosier's Ghost*, came out with an illustrative print (74). Walpole's return to his home county of Norfolk in the summer of 1733 produced both a ballad and a print on a theme derived from Butler's *Hudibras* (32). The excise crisis yielded one of the most famous of all eighteenth-century ballads. *Britannia Excisa* was produced in two parts and pirated in many versions. All of these appeared with pictures of Walpole first exulting and then lamenting as the crisis developed (23, 28). Similar co-ordination was practised with the newspapers. In a continuing controversy a cartoon offered a valuable variation on the main theme. One of the most vicious satires on the royal family, the irreverent *Festival of the Golden Rump*, arose directly from a prolonged period of barracking by the opposition newspapers, and was followed by elaborate explanations of the print in the press (48). A rare initiative from the government side was also inexplicable except as part of the war of words. A court supporter had accused the *Craftsman* of seeking to 'tinker' with the constitution. The *Craftsman* unwisely took objection to this language and the result was a telling cartoon in which the paper's editor, Nicholas Amhurst, was pictured as a travelling tinker (71). Only those familiar with the pieces in the press would have fully appreciated the point being made.

Of necessity the prints were concerned with the main lines of the case against Walpole's system, rather than with the subtler shades of argument. That case was provided readily by the opposition press, and most notably by the *Craftsman*. Its central contention, that Whig oligarchy and corruption were destroying the British constitution, was predictably the chief concern of the engravers. Walpole himself characteristically appears in the prints dispensing bribes financed by an overburdened, tax-paying public (60). In *Britannia Excisa* the monster excise regurgitates gold into the minister's lap (23); in another print, Walpole is carried along on his money chest remorselessly grinding taxes from the people (84). He is often accompanied by revenue officers – the exciseman especially, with his measuring scales or gauge is a frequent, sinister attendant (34, 84). The recipients of the booty are also displayed. No opportunity is lost to comment on Walpole's corruption of the church (obliquely in 45, more specifically in 84), the legal profession (83) and above all the politicians (87), and the electorate (80, 84). Fear of prosecution ensured that few views of Parliament itself were offered, and hardly any of what went on in the House of Commons. But discrete hints were given. The exterior of Westminster Hall is shown, with the weather vane pointing in Walpole's direction (22). In one cartoon, which could afford to be bold, because it actually followed Walpole's fall, the minister is shown controlling the M.P.s, puppet-like in their seats in the House (104). But more generally Walpolian M.P.s appear as easily identifiable courtiers or camp followers, corrupting electors with gold, and office (5, 84), or, most vividly, crawling through the mire of corruption with their leader (80). Wherever possible, the standing army (after the general charge of corruption, the most popular item in the list of Walpole's offences) is introduced, supporting the excise (22, 24), or protecting Walpole from richly deserved punishment (83, 84, 87). The navy, by contrast, and following the practice of the patriot press, is always pictured as the unhappy but valorous victim of Walpole's policies, and the sailor as courageous, loyal and patriotic (56, 57, 58, 61, 63). A national disaster like Cartagena in 1741 provided an opportunity simultaneously to blame the army and exonerate the navy.

Charges such as these were familiar elements in the 'country' programme. That they were worked up in this period into such a powerful weapon against Hanoverian government owed much to the character which the prime minister himself imposed on his regime. Walpole, after all, was something of a gift for the satirist. His own unabashed delight in the accumulation of riches and honours, however gained, provided a ready target. His pride in the garter which he had taken in preference to a peerage was in itself natural enough. A peerage would have removed him to the relative impotence of the Lords and would inevitably have been followed by the appearance of a rival in the Commons. At the same time the award of the garter, the first to a commoner, made clear his pre-eminence at court and in the government. But it was a weapon easily turned against him, and among the symbols used to identify him in the prints none is more familiar or frequent than the sash of the order, described in the ballads as the blue ribbon or 'blew string'. Walpole also had a reputation for endorsing and protecting corruption even at the lowest levels. Independent-minded contemporaries who did not necessarily share the popular prejudice against all courtiers felt bound to admit to a certain distaste for Walpole's attachment to low and corrupt men. In the series of financial scandals which occurred in the early 1730s Walpole repeatedly intervened to preserve unsavoury associates from the vengeance of the Commons. Why he did so even in cases where he had no political interest involved remains something of a mystery. Most probably it reflected his frequently expressed dislike of political prosecutions by Parliament. His early years in politics had witnessed the exceptionally ferocious party strife of Queen Anne's reign and had not suggested the relatively civilised approach to political differences which historians now associate with the eighteenth century. He had himself suffered in 1712 from the tendency of the legislature to use its judicial or quasi-judicial powers for political purposes and in the 1730s seems genuinely to have feared that like first ministers before him he would end by being impeached. (His own conduct in arraigning Atterbury in Parliament in 1723 seemed inconsistent in this context, but Walpole always distinguished clearly between the treason of Jacobite conspiracy against the Protestant succession and the mis-demeanours involved in petty corruption.) Whatever the reason his apparent defence of fraud and corruption was well known. He could hardly complain then, when one of these scandals, that arising from the affairs of the Charitable Corporation, featured in a hostile print (*39*). On the other hand, at times he was clearly the victim of unjustified innuendo. He defended the arrangements by which the South Sea Company extended its trade with Spanish America on the plausible grounds that despite their illegality under the terms of the Treaty of Utrecht they were obviously in the national interest. For this he was depicted as corruptly abetting the Directors of the Company in defrauding the stockholders (*21*). Still more controversial was his involvement by the patriot propagandists in the Charteris affair. There is no evidence that Walpole was responsible for the king's pardon of a convicted rapist and notorious libertine but it was easy to assume that he was, and equally easy to exploit the supposed parallel between the sexual misdeeds of Colonel Charteris and the political misdeeds of the prime minister (*11, 13*). In this as in other matters Walpole's personal immorality did not help his cause. Had he been more circumspect, even more hypocritical, he might have been less exposed to criticism. But his very openness made him an easy target. In one print (*41*) he is attended by prostitutes, in others by his illegitimate daughter Maria Churchill. In one instance the latter is seen offering herself to the king (*102*), in another there is the clear implication that she was sexually familiar with Walpole himself (*99*).

George II's own character made matters worse. The king's unfortunate personal habits, his violent temper, his supposed liking for kicking both his hat and his domestics, above all his sexual promiscuity, reinforced the low opinion of his court and his ministers. The king appears with his mistresses in scenes in which no opportunity is lost to exploit the obscenities (*55, 96, 102*). The resulting picture of court and ministry merely reinforced the prevailing sense of illegitimacy which attached itself to the Hanoverian government. At a time when a considerable body of landowners and of the nation as a whole regarded George II as the lesser but also the less legitimate of two evils and the Walpolian system of government as a grossly improper violation of tradition, this important impression of essential illegitimacy was readily transmitted and easily recognised.

Two phases stand out in the development of a systematic campaign against Walpole, the excise crisis of 1733–4, and the controversies preceding the War of Jenkins' Ear and the War of the Austrian Succession. In each case the line taken was heavily dependent on the contemporary literature. The excise cartoons naturally concentrated on championing the cause of trade and prosperity against bureaucratic taxation and tyranny. Though fraudulent traders could only lose by Walpole's proposals for a more thorough revenue service, they were displayed to the public as the true beneficiaries (*24*), with Walpole himself, the army and the placemen (*22, 24*). The same predictable need to turn a complicated debate into a simple parade of the opposition's main charges was displayed five years later. Sensible attempts to compromise with Spain over the competing interests of British and Spanish trade in the Caribbean were shown as selling England down the river. The cause of Jenkins' Ear and the alleged mistreatment of the British by Spanish coastguards were easy subjects for the engraver; prints abounded in pathetic pictures of English merchants and sailors assaulted, tortured, imprisoned by the Spaniard (*57, 58*). Always in the background the British lion, the British tar or the British navy is restrained from action by Walpole's policy of peace at any price (*56, 61, 75*). Once war had begun, Walpole was depicted as at best an incompetent, at worst a traitorous war leader whose only consistent success lay in preventing the royal navy from coming to grips with the enemy fleet (*78, 81*). Pictorial defences of his strategy were rare, and lack conviction (*65*). Even the victory of Portobello was quickly registered as an opposition rather than a national triumph, and the victor Admiral Vernon, a friend of Pulteney, made an asset for the 'patriot' side (*72, 73, 74, 93, 94*). Vernon was involved in the disgraceful failure at Cartagena, but for that Walpole was held personally responsible (*94, 95*).

The volume of the prints dealing with Walpole's foreign policy is a measure of the progress made by the political cartoon in this period. But these prints formed only part of an extraordinary outburst of graphic polemic in the years preceding Walpole's fall. It is possible to trace the process by which Walpole's political position weakened and fully disintegrated in some detail. Increasingly strained relations between George II and his son, leading to Prince Frederick's junction with the opposition in 1737, were reflected in one print concerned with the birth of the Prince's first child (*49*). The Prince's desertion was to play an important part in Walpole's downfall, both by stimulating further defections from the court, and by reducing the government's majority in the general election of 1741. Almost as important was the loss of Walpole's principal Scottish ally, the Duke of Argyll. Argyll's decision to join the Prince in opposition in 1740 was a fearful blow to the government's normally safe majority in Scotland; the cartoonists showed themselves well aware of its significance (*68, 76*). They were also alert to less important discordancies in the Walpole system. The quarrel between the prime minister and his 'pope' – Gibson of London – was a case in point. Walpole's success in stifling religion as a political issue had depended on simultaneously pacifying the fears of the ecclesiastical establishment and quieting the clamour of the dissenters. In 1735 renewed agitation for reform among the latter and a small but disturbing outbreak of anti-clericalism in the House of Commons provoked Gibson to break the truce of many years and left Walpole stranded. The prints inevitably but inaccurately portrayed Gibson as a latter-day Laud (*43, 44*). These diverse comments on political developments revealed clearly that by the late 1730s, the opposition and its Grub Street friends had successfully established a new and enduring weapon in practical politics, capable of responding to the issues as they arose. The *Motion* series, though occasioned by a notable opposition failure (the defeat of the Commons motion for Walpole's removal in February 1741), and initiated by the friends of government, was belated but highly effective recognition of this addition to the political armoury. It also constituted a novelty in itself – the first full-scale dialogue commenced, sustained and dominated by the cartoonist rather than the pamphleteer or journalist.

IV.
The Impact of the Prints

In these as in other controversies the prints closely followed the drift of anti-ministerial thinking and tactics generally. It is this dependence of the graphic satire on the press which makes it particularly difficult to assess its relative impact and importance. Quite apart from the general impracticability of weighing the precise effect of polemic on public opinion, the auxiliary role of the prints deprives them of the originality in debate and argument which at least distinguishes some literary forms of satire. In consequence the distinctive importance of the prints is to be found more in the character of their audience than in the nature of their subjects.

In most respects, it must be admitted, the market for the prints lay with the market for the products of Grub Street generally, that is to say the great mass of middling people involved in trade, industry or the emerging professions, who had both the resources and the literacy to take an interest in the products of the press. Particularly in London such people constituted a substantial section of society, stretching between the polite and propertied who formed the ruling class and the plebeians who in theory at least possessed no political role at all. The newspapers, pamphlets, even ballads which emerged at an increasing rate from Grub Street were necessarily concerned with the doings of the rulers, and were in some measure dependent upon them. But without this great body of 'middling' opinion in both the capital and the provinces there would have been no audience for the newly established popular press and no enlightened public opinion of the kind which even the most corrupt and cynical of oligarchical politicians knew to exist. Whether a market could be found in the classes below the middling sort was more problematical. The prints, in particular, were not cheap. They cost more than most ballads and as much as many pamphlets. Even for a poorly produced woodcut or pirated copper-plate engraving, 6d was the standard charge. *The Motion* was most unusual in selling at 4d and perhaps owed something of its great popularity to this fact. At prices of this order there could certainly be no question of a mass market for the prints beyond that which customarily purchased books and newspapers.

Nonetheless, the audience for the prints had two distinctive features. In the first place London effectually monopolised the business of producing cartoons. The dominance of the metropolis is, of course, a feature of the eighteenth-century press generally. But by the 1730s, most important provincial towns had their own printers, and many were producing their own newspapers, in addition to acting as distribution centres for the London press. Even this degree of provincial autonomy could not apply to the production of graphic work, however. Engraving needed a printing press of quite different design from the letter-press. The technology was not particularly new, but it remained a separate and expensive investment. The purchase of a rolling press for the production of copperplate engraving, let alone any of the more sophisticated new techniques of mezzotint and aquatint was beyond most general printers. Consequently the engravers were necessarily concentrated heavily in the capital and their products sold in the provinces only by the slightly cumbersome means available for the distribution of London publications generally. This made little difference to the availability of the more elaborate and lavish engraving, on a devotional or artistic subject. But it probably affected the market for topical and political prints and thereby made the London audience still more dominating. It is not surprising, for instance, that the few prints which concerned specific parliamentary elections related to constituencies in or near London. Thus the controversy surrounding the Westminster election of 1741 was readily exploited and exaggerated far beyond its relative importance (*91, 92*); no provincial election, however important, would have been so easy to picture and interpret for a metropolitan audience.

A second distinction was also important. By definition the newspapers and pamphlets, and the ballads at least in the first instance, were designed for the literate. But the cartoons were in principle comprehensible by a much wider audience. They were displayed in the print shops where it was customary to arrange the latest prints in the window, as well as in the coffee house and ale house where they could be seen on the walls. This fact opened up an important new section of the public to political debate. The fascination of the metropolitan lower orders with political news and gossip was a feature of English life which never failed to astonish continental visitors.[16] The prints played a part in the political education of these classes and exploded any hope that the political battles of the 1730s could be kept within the ranks of the wealthy and the educated. It was precisely this implied appeal that concerned many contemporaries, for it encouraged questioning, irreverence, and even opposition among those classes of whom unquestioning acceptance was expected. 'Prints are a universal Language, understood by Persons of all Nations and Degrees. He that runs may read . . . Every Window of every Printshop is in a Manner glazed, and the Shop itself papered with Libels.'[17]

With these distinctions in mind it is possible to isolate something of the special effect of the prints. The effect had less to do with the statement of arguments against Walpole, than with the images inspired and prejudices stirred. Certain things of this kind could not be done in the more conventional press. For example the violence and extremism which lay not far below the surface in national politics were sensitive matters for the journalists. Walpole, who genuinely seems to have feared prosecution or impeachment, was often threatened with both by his opponents in the press. But direct incitements to violence were dangerously imprudent, and the opposition journals relied heavily on the use of historical parallels and analogies to suggest the possible fate of wicked ministers like Walpole. Such references were fully understood by their readers. They remained, however, indirect and in the last analysis somewhat ineffective. Translated into visual form, their implications could be made much clearer. The historical parallels were much used here too, but the pictures which accompanied them were far from historical. The print which showed a corpse being carried away for mutilation and burning, bore captions suggesting that Sejanus or the De Witt brothers were intended (*34*). The picture itself unmistakably showed Walpole's body with a band of attendant excisemen. The hangman's noose and the executioner's axe are familiar features of such prints (*35, 52*). The block was specified with proper accuracy after Walpole became a peer in 1742 (*105*). Like the prints in which Walpole and his associates are shown in coarse, brutal, obscene, or otherwise offensive attitudes or postures, they exploited the priceless asset of the graphic satire and demonstrated, perhaps paradoxically, that what could not be put unequivocally in prose, might readily be presented pictorially with the added advantage that its significance was obvious to a mean and illiterate audience.

The relevance of the prints to specifically popular politics can also be seen in terms of the imagery employed by the engraver. There was, most notably, a strong and continuing connection between the world of the political cartoonist and the world of popular theatre. Politics and the theatre were indeed frequently found in collusion or conflict in the 1730s. The sensation caused, slightly to its author's surprise, by Gay's *Beggar's Opera*, was followed by a protracted war between the authorities and the theatre managers, involving the proscription of authors and plays, and eventually, in 1737, censorship by statute. One of the reasons why the theatrical mode of criticism was so powerful was that it reinforced a popular belief that the existing regime was by its very nature in a sense false, deceiving and theatrical. This sense was also conveyed, and to a wider audience, in the prints. Walpole and his friends were regularly shown as conjurors, magicians or wizards, employing cheap tricks to deceive the populace (*14, 48*). They appeared also as raree-showmen, charlatans and quacks, and no aspect of the burlesque was neglected in the opposition's highly successful attempt to deny Walpole precisely the standing and substance which he claimed (*32*). Punch (*40*), harlequins (*14, 60*), puppets (*104*), jugglers (*64*), all suggested the bogus and the meretricious in Walpole's domestic and diplomatic policies. Even the screen, much employed by artists to depict the public evils of the Hanoverian system on its face, and to reveal the private corruption which it concealed behind, was a theatrical metaphor (*4, 5, 104, 105*). Parliament itself, after the general election of 1734, was shown as an elaborate farce with an appropriate play-bill to herald its sitting (*40*). This artistic campaign reached an appropriate climax with the disillusionment which followed Walpole's eventual fall in 1742. Walpole himself was protected from prosecution, his old enemies removed the mask of the patriot to reveal the face of a hypocrite (*103*), and the entire political scene was reduced to a kind of theatrical farce – the *Magna Farta* of state, in which the king himself became a contemptuous and contemptible showman, manipulating all who played any part in public life (*108*).

The importance of the cartoons of the Walpole era is more likely to be found in this, the way in which they sustained and reinforced public prejudices and popular participation in politics, especially in London itself, than in any artistic achievement. Without Hogarth there was indeed little to distinguish the cartoonists themselves.

Francis Hayman could be seen as a major figure in his own right, and some of his colleagues who began to sign their work in the 1730s, Peter Fourdrinier, Gerard Vandergucht, Gerard Scotin, and the Bickmans, could lay claims to a modest eminence. But the work for which such men were later praised was rarely their political satire. Typical in this respect is the verdict of Joseph Strutt, the first serious student of engraving to make a critical evaluation. Scotin, for instance, he dismissed as 'an industrious man; but his prints do no credit to his taste'. Discussing Fourdrinier, he was moved to observe: 'It was a happy circumstance for the artists of this class, that the taste of their employers was not more refined, otherwise they would, without doubt, have considered their engravings as a disgrace, rather than an ornament, to any creditable publication'.[18] The essence of the political cartoon was its topicality, and topicality militated against excellence. Printers and engravers were expected to produce, at short notice, work which they could neither prepare nor develop in full. Printers, especially, were apt to publish as cheaply and shoddily as possible. Hogarth's description of the trade stressed the depressing way in which artists of genuine merit would inevitably see their work sold below its value, or imitated and mass-produced by inferior engravers. There was a strong sense in the 1720s and 1730s of the great pressure placed on the publishing and printing business by the apparently inexhaustible demand for the products of the press (20). Pirating was, of course, widespread, and the mere process of copying was bound to lower artistic standards. Even a woodcut as humble as *Britannia Excisa* which began with a lively and engaging picture of Walpole quickly degenerated in the process of reproduction (23, 28). Reputable artists were encouraged to cut costs and corners; for example, the re-use and re-working of old plates was a frequent expedient (94). No amount of retrospective assessment can rescue the artistic reputation of those involved. It is perhaps one of the minor ironies of the age of Hogarth that the historical interest of the satirical engraving lies so much in its political impact and so little in its aesthetic quality.

FOOTNOTES

1. *Walpole Soc.*, XXX, p.199
2. Ibid. pp.197–8
3. *Walpole Soc.*, XVIII, p.15
4. In a vast literature a recent and most helpful study is R. Paulson, *Hogarth's Graphic Works* (New Haven and London, 2 vols., 1965); a much shorter, but admirably clear introduction is F. D. Klingender, *Hogarth and English Caricature* (New York, 1944).
5. See J. Burke and C. Caldwell, *Hogarth: The Complete Engravings* (London 1968), Plate 16.
6. It is frequently assumed that Hogarth had a strong, if unexpressed, sympathy with the opposition. This tradition seems to owe more to the concern of his biographers to disassociate him from the Walpole regime than to any hard evidence of his views.
7. For an account of Hogarth's relations with Wilkes, see P. Quennell, *Hogarth's Progress* (London, 1955), chap. xiv.
8. See J. Burke, *Hogarth and Reynolds: A Contrast in English Art Theory* (London, 1943).
9. See R. Paulson, *Emblem and Expression: Meaning in English Art of the Eighteenth Century.*
10. See below, p.29.
11. For example see, on shop signs, A. Heal, *The Signboards of Old London Shops* (London, 1947), and on tradesmen's cards, A. Heal, *London Tradesmen's Cards of the XVIII Century* (London, 1925).
12. H. M. Atherton, *Political Prints in the Age of Hogarth* (Oxford, 1974), pp. 75, 69, 71.
13. 'A Voyage to Laputa [etc.]', Book vi.
14. The ambiguity of this print has given rise to controversy. Stephens and H. M. Atherton (op. cit., p.45) treat it as an intended panegyric, M. D. George, *English Political Caricature to 1792* (Oxford 1959), as a satire.
15. For ballads generally in this period, see M. Percival, ed. *Political Ballads Illustrating the Administration of Sir Robert Walpole*, Oxford, 1916. See also J. Holloway and J. Black, *Later English Broadside Ballads* (London, 1975).
16. See, for example, Madame Van Muyden, ed. *A Foreign View of England in the Reigns of George I and George II. The Letters of Monsieur César de Saussure to His Family* (London, 1906), p.162.
17. *Public Advertiser*, 5 June 1765.
18. J. Strutt, *A Biographical Dictionary: containing an historical account of all the engravers, . . .* (London, 2 vols., 1785–6), II. p.312, I. p.304.

THE PLATES

The following points should be noted.

a) The number of the print appears initially in each caption.

b) The B.M.C. number given in each case refers to the *Catalogue of prints and drawings in the British Museum, Division 1, Political and personal satires* ed. F. G. Stephen, E. Hawkins, M. D. George, 1870–, which should be consulted for a fuller explanation.

c) The date is that of publication when it appears on the print or when it is ascertainable by other means. Dates suggested on the basis of external evidence or the topicality of the print appear within square brackets.

d) The engraver and/or designer are specified wherever possible. Before the copyright act of 1735 such attributions are extremely difficult; even after that date they are erratic and unreliable. The printer/publisher is not identified here.

e) The title of each print is not repeated. Where the print appeared originally as a frontispiece, or in company with a ballad or broadside, this is indicated in the description.

f) Many of the prints bear MS. additions identifying allusions, engravers, and so on. These are often unreliable.

1. BMC 1610 [1720]

   The mania for speculation was international and the cards show the Dutch and French versions as well as the South Sea Bubble itself in England. Most of the satires published on this subject originated on the Continent.

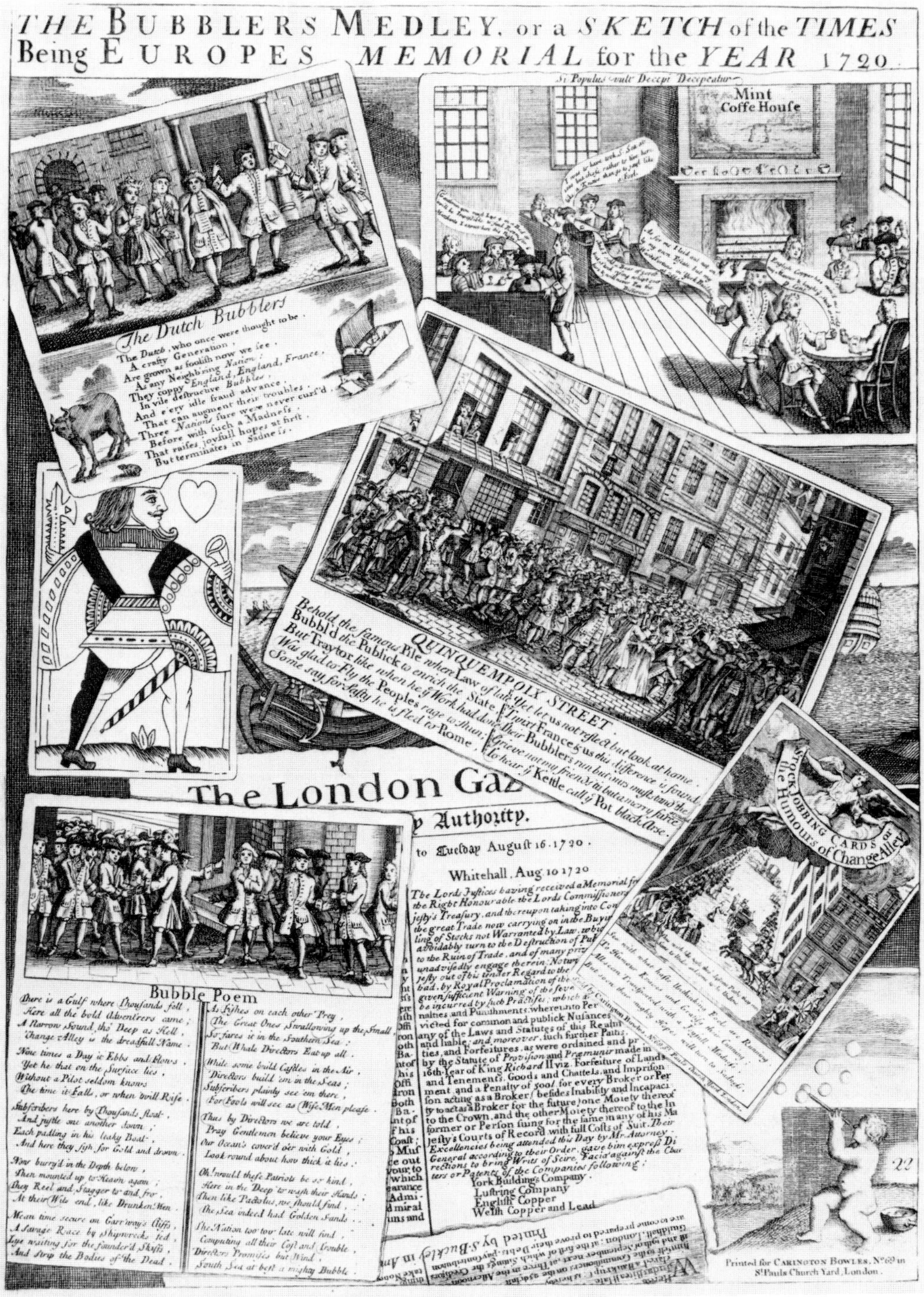
THE BUBBLERS MEDLEY, or a SKETCH of the TIMES
Being EUROPES MEMORIAL for the YEAR 1720.
Si Populus vult Decepi Decepeatur
Mint Coffe House
The Dutch Bubblers
The Dutch, who once were thought to be,
A crafty Generation,
Are grown as foolish now we see,
As any Neighb'ring Nation;
They coppy England, England, France,
In vile destructive Bubbles,
And e'ery idle fraud advance,
That can augment their troubles.
Three Nations sure were never curs'd,
Before with such a Madness,
That raises joyfull hopes at first,
But terminates in Sadness.
QUINQUEMPOIX STREET.
Behold the famous Pile where Law of late, Yet let us not reflect but look at home,
Bubbl'd the Publick to enrich the State, 'Twixt France & us this difference is found,
But Traytor like when he ye Work had done Their Bubblers run but ours must stand the
Was glad to Fly the Peoples rage to shun; Grieve not my friends tis but a merry farce
Some say for Safety he is fled to Rome. To hear ye Kettle call ye Pot black Arse.
Stock-Jobbing Cards or the Humours of Change Alley
The London Gaz
y Authority.
to Tuesday August 16. 1720.
Whitehall, Aug. 10 1720
The Lords Justices having received a Memorial fr
the Right Honourable the Lords Commissioners
jesty's Treasury, and thereupon taking into Con
the great Trade now carrying on in the Buyi
ling of Stocks not Warranted by Law, whi
avoidably turn to the Destruction of Pu
to the Ruin of Trade, and of many priv
unadvisedly engage therein; Notwi
jesty out of his tender Regard to the
had, by Royal Proclamation of the
given sufficient Warning of the seve
be incurred by such Practises, which
nalties and Punishments whereunto Per
victed for common and publick Nusances
any of the Laws and Statutes of this Realm
and liable; and moreover, such further Pains
ties, and Forfeitures, as were ordained and pr
by the Statute of Provision and Præmunir made in
16th Year of King Richard II viz. Forfeiture of Lands
and Tenements, Goods and Chattels, and Imprison
ment, and a Penalty of 500l. for every Broker or Per
son acting as a Broker (besides Inability and Incapaci
ty to act as a Broker for the future) one Moiety thereof
to the Crown, and the other Moiety thereof to the In
former or Person suing for the same in any of his Ma
jesty's Courts of Record with full Costs of Suit. Their
Excellencies being attended this Day by Mr. Attorney
General according to their Order, gave him express Di
rections to bring Writs of Scire Facia against the Char
ters or Patents of the Companies following;
York Buildings Company.
Lustring Company
English Copper
Welsh Copper and Lead
Printed by S. Buckley in Am
Bubble Poem
There is a Gulf where Thousands fell,
Here all the bold Adventrers came;
A Narrow Sound, tho' Deep as Hell,
'Change Alley is the dreadfull Name.
Nine times a Day it Ebbs and Flows,
Yet he that on the Surface lies,
Without a Pilot seldom knows
The time it Falls, or when twill Rise.
Subscribers here by Thousands float,
And justle one another down,
Each padling in his leaky Boat,
And here they fish for Gold and drown.
Now burry'd in the Depth below,
Then mounted up to Heav'n again;
They Reel and Stagger to and fro,
At their Wits end, like Drunken Men.
Mean time secure on Garr'way's Cliffs,
A Savage Race by Shipwrecks fed,
Lye waiting for the founder'd Skiffs,
And Strip the Bodies of the Dead.
As Fishes on each other Prey,
The Great Ones Swallowing up the Small,
So fares it in the Southern Sea;
But Whale Directors Eat up all.
While some build Castles in the Air,
Directors build 'em in the Seas;
Subscribers plainly see 'em there,
For Fools will see as Wise Men please.
Thus by Directors we are told,
Pray Gentlemen believe your Eyes;
Our Ocean's cover'd o'er with Gold,
Look round about how thick it lies.
Oh! would these Patriots be so kind,
Here in the Deep to wash their Hands;
Then like Pactolus, we should find,
The Sea indeed had Golden Sands.
The Nation too too late will find,
Computing all their Cost and Trouble,
Directors Promises but Wind,
South Sea at best a mighty Bubble.
Printed for CARINGTON BOWLES, No. 69 in
St. Pauls Church Yard, London.

2. BMC 1620   [1720]

An informative presentation of the English Bubble. At each side are lists of the projects on offer to investors. Above, a variety of the projects are displayed around a wheel of fortune; below, a coat of arms bears bizarre emblems of chance and folly; in the centre is a complacent speculator.

The BUBLERS MIRROUR or ENGLAND'S FOLLEY

3. BMC 1722   [1721]   William Hogarth

    Hogarth's elaborate version of the South Sea Bubble. The roundabout in the centre is worked by the South Sea company directors, and is symbolically adjacent to the monument erected in memory of the destruction of the City in the Great Fire. Trade expires in a corner. In the left background women queue for a raffle for husbands. In the left foreground the devil cuts pieces of fortune's flesh and throws them to the crowd. Vice flourishes and virtue is laid low in the shape of various emblematic figures described by the caption. There is a tradition that the dwarf-like figure picking a pocket in the centre was meant for Alexander Pope.

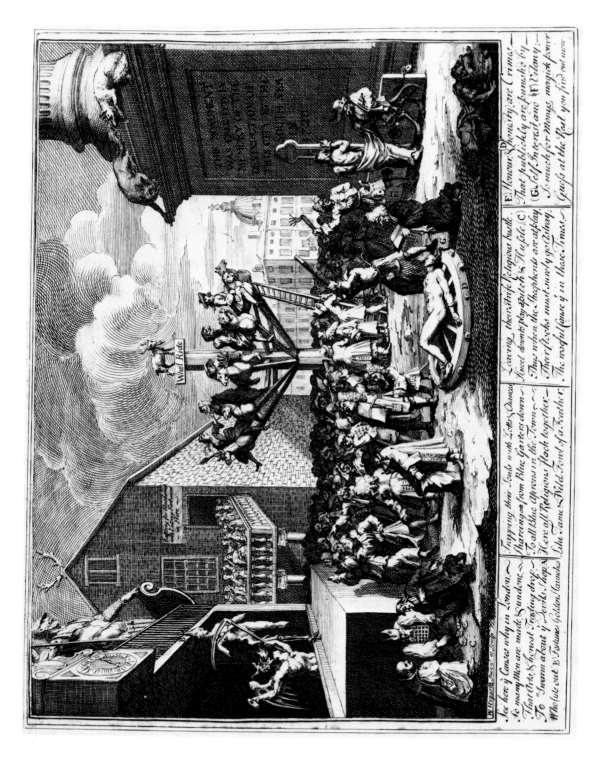

See here y Causes why in London. ~
So many Men are made Sundome ~
That Arts & honest Trading drop. ~
To Swarm about y Devil's Shop. ~
Who lose out B Fortune golden Nameha ~

Trapping their Souls with Lotto Chances ~
Sharcangon Blue Garters down ~
To all Blue Aprons in the Town ~
Here all Religions flock together ~
Like Jame Wild Fowl of a Feather. ~

Leaving their strife Religious bustle ~
Kneel down to play, Bspitch & Hustle. (C)
Thus when the Shepherds are at play,
Their Flocks must surely go Astray ~
The woful Cause y in these Times, ~

E) Honour; & honesty, are Crimes
That publickly are bumch'd by
(G) Self Interest and (F) Villany:
So much for monys magick power
Guess at the Rest you find out now

W. Hogarth Inv.t et Sculp.

4. BMC 1712   [1721]

The villain of the piece, Robert Knight, cashier of the South Sea Company, fled to Belgium and was there protected from prosecution by the legal privileges (the 'Joyeuse Entree') of the estates of Brabant. On the left Knight receives a safe conduct from George I's mistress, the Duchess of Kendal. On the other side a mirror reveals the screeners, presumably Walpole, the Duchess and the king's other favourite, Charlotte von Kielmansegg. The screen itself presents various cynical views of the Bubble.

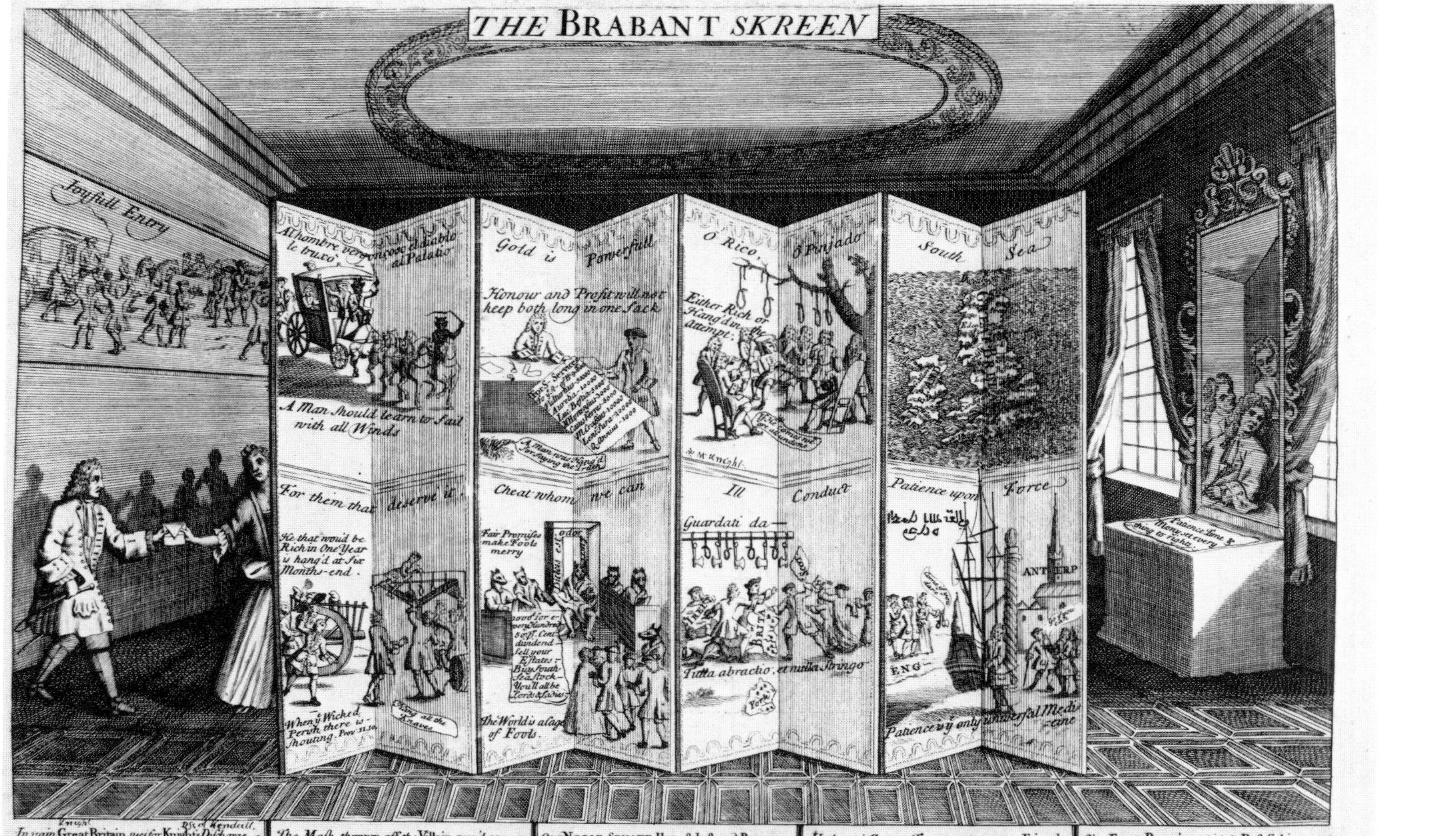
THE BRABANT SKREEN
Joyfull Entry
Al hombre vergonçoso el diablo le truxo al Palatio
A Man should learn to sail with all Winds
For them that deserve it.
He that would be Rich in One Year is hang'd at Six Months-end
When the Wicked Perish there is Shouting. Prov. 11.10
Gold is Powerfull
Honour and Profit will not keep both long in one Sack
A Man was hang'd for saying the Truth
Cheat whom we can
Fair Promises make Fools merry
The World is a Cage of Fools.
O Rico, ó Enjado
Either Rich or Hang'd in the attempt.
Ill Conduct
Guardati da —
Tutta abractio; et nulla Stringo
South Sea
Patience upon Force
ANTWERP
ENG—
Patience is ye only universal Medicine

Knight Bp. of Kendell

In vain, Great Britain *sues for* Knight's *Discharge*, —
In vain we hope *to see that* Wretch *at large!* —
If Traitors *here, the* Villain *there secure*,
Our Ills *must all encrease, our* Woes *be sure*.
Should he Return, ye SCREEN *would useless be*,
And all Men then the Mystery *would see*;

The Mask thrown off, the Villain *would appear*
Not Antwerp's *Slave, but* Others *that are here*. —
ALMIGHTY GOD, *exert thy* Awful Power, —
Oh! let not Sycophants *our Land devour*: —
Too sure again! we may be All *betray'd*,
If to do Justice *now, we are afraid!* —

Our NOBLE SENATE, Honest Just, *and* Brave, —
Fain would This Realm *from dire* Destruction *save*.
They ALL UNITE, *Our* GLORY *to inflame*,
And would confirm *us* GREAT, *as is our* Name!
Too well They see those Snakes, *who perdue lie*
SCREEN'D *by Betrayers of our Liberty*.
Who bask themselves in that Security. —

Under this Covert *They would seem our* Friends
But Oh! Their treach'rous Aims *have fatal* Ends
Assist GREAT GEORGE *ye* Reins *of* Empires *Thine*
Guide Thou thy Chariot, *like a* God Divine! —
Let no curs'd Traitor *tho of* High Degree —
Eclipse the Beams of Sacred Majesty! —

Give Ear to PRAY'RS *which thy* Best Subjects *make*,
And, oh! defend *this* Land *for* Pity's *sake*.
Each Member *of ye* State, *distinctly* Brave,
Does, by Addressing *thy* Protection *crave*:
Throughout ye Realm, *our loud* Complaints *are* sent.
Oh KING & FATHER! *All our* Griefs prevent!

Mr Knight imprisoned at Antwerp the Brabant States objected to give him up to England and thereby SKREENED him.

London Journal Numb. 92 Ap. 29 1721

5. BMC 1717   [1722]

The general election of 1722. The screen bears the most unpopular statutes of the previous parliament, including the hated Septennial Act. The mirror reflects ministers skulking behind the screen. A candidate emerges to bribe a member of the corporation; the latter's wife is persuaded of the propriety of the bribe by a clergyman. The boys point the moral with a wooden shoe, the traditional emblem of French slavery. Walpole's parliamentary majority was consolidated by the election.

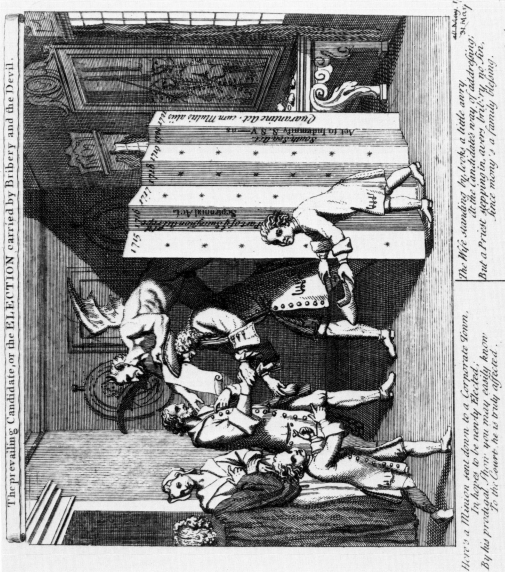

The prevailing Candidate, or the ELECTION carried by Bribery and the Devil.

Here's a Minion sent down to a Corporate Town,
In hopes to be nicely Elected;
By his prodigal Show, you may easily know
To the Court he is truly affected.

He is a Knave by the hand, who has pow'r to command,
till the Votes in the Corporation;
Shove a saint in his pocket, the Devil cries take it,
'Tis all for the good of the Nation.

The Mifs standing by, looks a little awry
at the Candidate's way of addressing;
But a Priest slipping in, avers 'tis no Sin,
since money's a family Blessing.

Say if Irops yet sad Rogues here are french woodenbrogues
To reward your vile breacherous Knav'ry;
For such Traitors as you, are the Rascally Crew
That betrays the whole Kingdom to Slav'ry.

See Smollett £ 2. ch. 11. Sec.

6. BMC 1749   [1724]

The extension to Ireland of England's corruption. William Wood's patent to supply the Irish with much needed copper coins was denounced by Swift as Hanoverian jobbery and presented as an invasion of the Dublin Parliament's rights. Here the coins are shown arriving, bringing poverty in their wake. Mercury descends, Hibernia laments the fate of her country and the true wealth of Ireland is carried off for shipment to England. The agitation was sufficient to force the abandonment of the project.

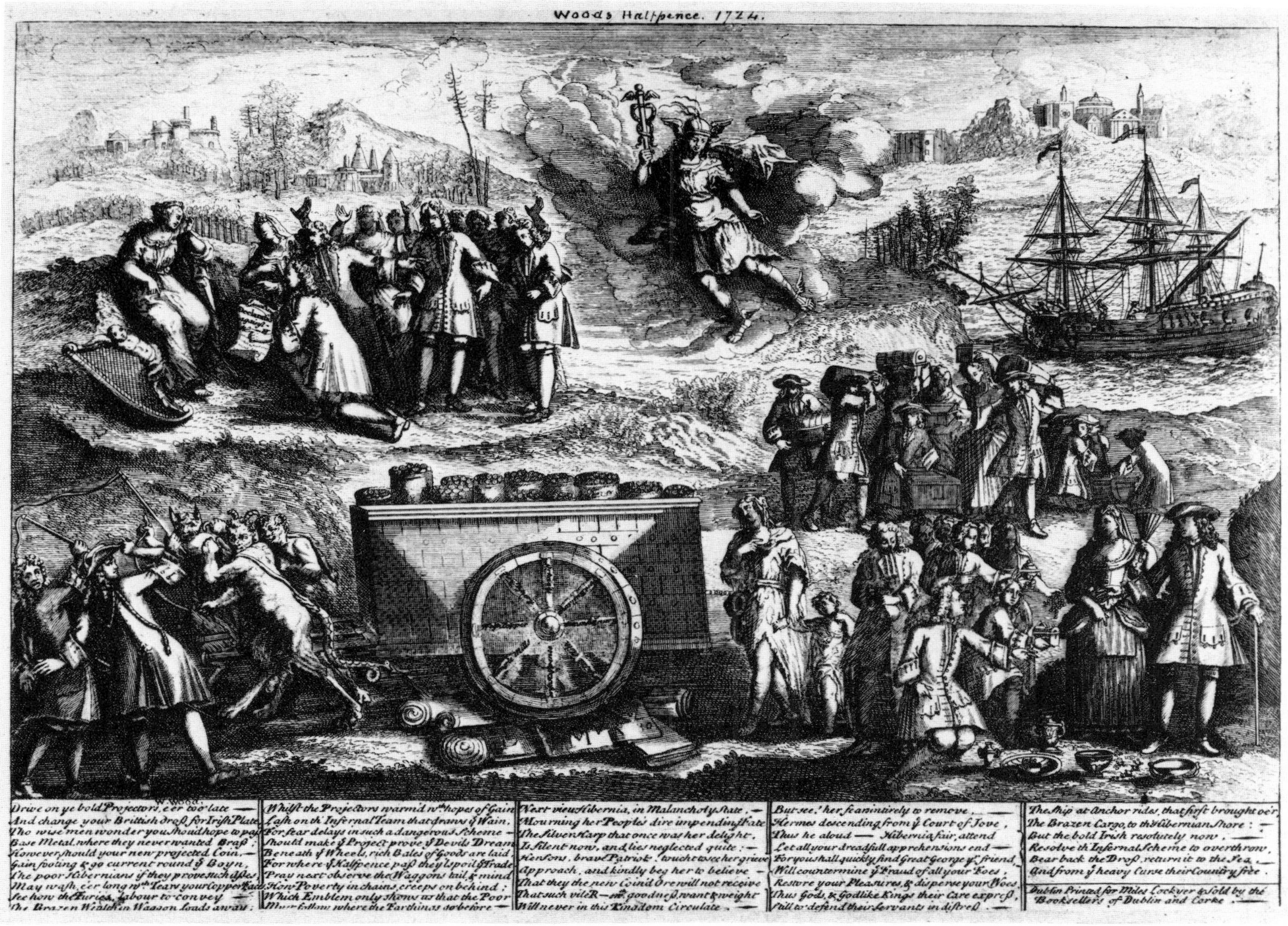
Woods Halfpence. 1724.
W. Wood.
Drive on ye bold Projectors, e'er too late —
And change your Brittish dross for Irish Plate
Tho wise men wonder you shoud hope to pass
Base Metal, where they never wanted Brass;
However, should your new projected Coin, —
Gain footing & go current round ye Boyn,
The poor Hibernians if they prove such Asses,
May wash, e'er long wth. Tears your Copper Faces
See how the Furies, labour to convey —
The Brazen Wealth in Waggon loads away;
Whilst the Projectors warm'd wth. hopes of Gain
Lash on th' Infernal Team that draws ye Wain,
For fear delays in such a dangerous Scheme —
Should make ye Project prove ye Devils Dream
Beneath ye Wheels, rich Bales of Goods are laid,
For where ye Halfpence pass they spoil ye Trade
Pray next observe the Waggons tail, & mind
How Poverty in chains, creeps on behind;
Which Emblem only shews us that the Poor
Must follow where the Farthings go before —
Next view Hibernia, in Malancholy State, —
Mourning her People's dire impending Fate
The Silver Harp that once was her delight,
Is silent now, and lies neglected quite: —
Hensons, brave Patriot, trucht to see her grieve
Approach, and kindly beg her to believe —
That they the new Coin'd Ore will not receive
That such vile R—sm. goodness, want & weight
Will never in this Kingdom Circulate. —
But see! her fears intirely to remove —
Hermes descending from ye Court of Jove,
Thus he aloud — Hibernia fair, attend
Let all your dreadfull apprehensions end —
For you shall quickly find Great George yr. friend,
Will countermine ye Fraud of all your Foes,
Restore your Pleasures, & disperse your Woes,
Thus Gods, & Godlike Kings their Care express,
Still to defend their Servants in distress. —
The Ship at Anchor rides, that first brought o'er,
The Brazen Cargo, to th' Hibernian Shore: —
But the bold Irish resolutely now, —
Resolve th' Infernal Scheme to overthrow,
Bear back the Dross, return it to the Sea, —
And from ye heavy Curse their Country free.
Dublin Printed for Miles Cockver & sold by the Booksellers of Dublin and Corke. —

7. BMC 1734   [December 1724]   William Hogarth
    Hogarth's sinister, almost surreal depiction of English government. Enthroned
    with their attendants are the monarchy, the church and the law.

Some of the Principal Inhabitants of yͤ MOON, as they
Were Perfectly Discover'd by a Telescope brought to yͤ Greatest
Perfection since yͤ last Eclipse; Exactly Engraved from the
Objects, whereby yͤ Curious may Guess at their Religion,
Manners, &c.

1725.   Price Six Pence.

8. BMC 1797   [December 1726]   William Hogarth
    Hogarth's version of a scene from the newly-published *Gulliver's Travels*.
    Gulliver, having put out a fire in the royal palace by urinating on it, is subjected
    to humiliating retaliation at the hands of the unappreciative Lilliputians. It was
    thus the fate of a patriotic critic of government to pay dearly for his well-
    intentioned and salutary advice.

THE POLITICAL CLYSTER

A Ms Hop. the Wmtn'sts apt's ki ki. shal k Fignl. Ser Gulliver's speech to the Hon. House of Nob, in Lilliput.

9. BMC 1798   [1727]
   The general election of 1727. Statues of folly and justice gaze down on a scene of universal corruption in a country borough.

Ready Mony the prevailing Candidate, or the Humours of an Election. 727

10. BMC 1857   [c.1730]
    Walpole portrayed as the second Julius Caesar, threatening a new dictatorship,
    to the alarm of his English audience.

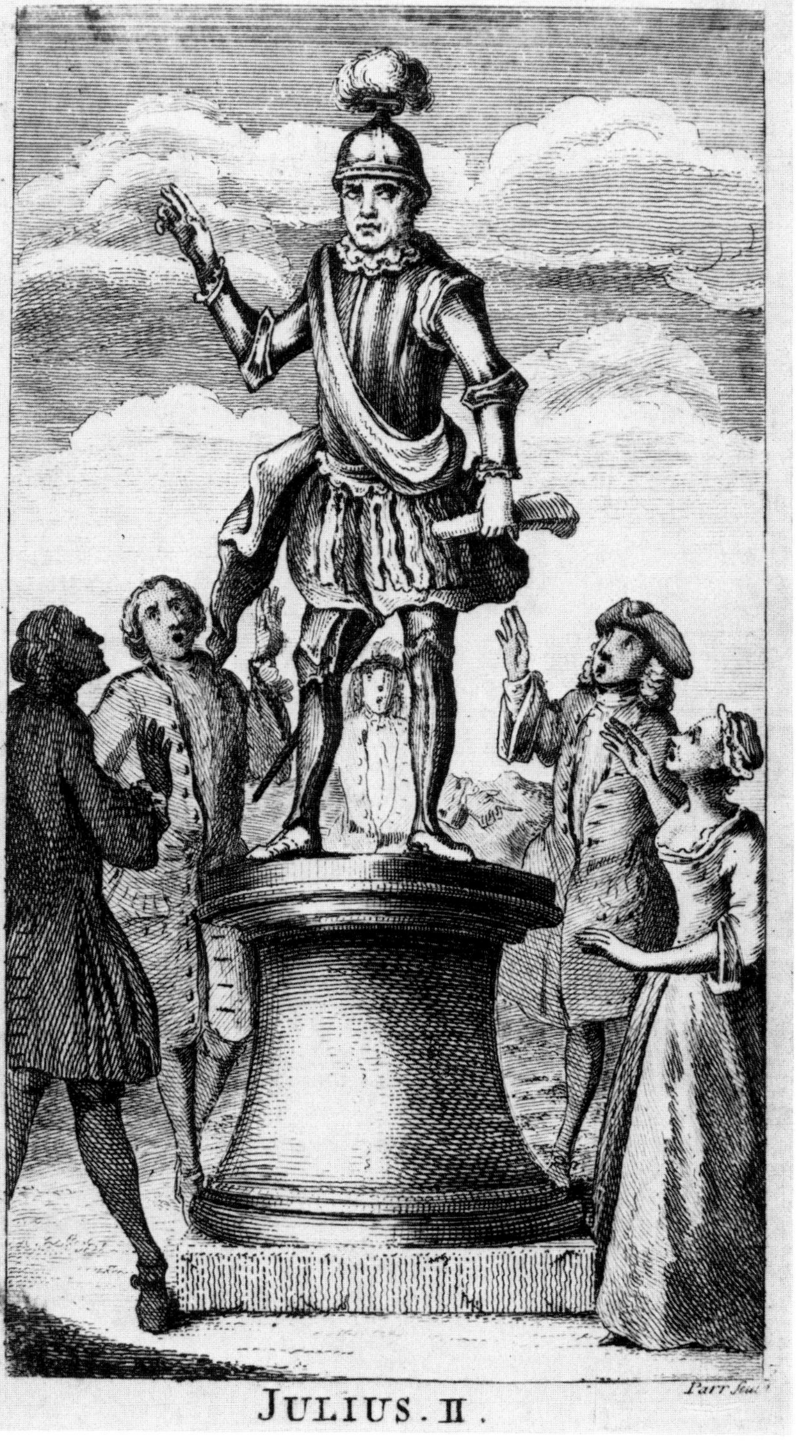

Parr Sculp.

JULIUS. II.

11. BMC 1840   [1730]

A rare character study, exploiting the popular interest in the sensational trial of Colonel Francis Charteris. Charteris was a notorious rake, convicted of the rape of a serving girl but pardoned by the king. His immunity provoked a bitter debate about the favour shown by English law to the wealthy and privileged.

COLONEL FRANCISCO.

Blood! must a Colonel with a Lords Estate   Shall they b'accountable to Saucy Juries——
Be thus obnoxious to a Scoundrels fate?   For this or t'other pleasure?—H—ll & Furies!
Brought to the Bar, & Sentenc'd from y' Bench   What man thro' Villainy would run a Course,
For only Ravishing a Country Wench?   And ruin Families without remorse
Shall Gentlemen receive no more respect?   To heap up Riches—if when all is done
Shall their Diversions thus by Laws be check'd?   An ignominious Death he cannot Shun?

12. BMC 1842 [June 1730] Designed F. Dumouchel and J. Faget; engraved P. Fourdrinier.

A panegyric, possibly intended ironically. Walpole ascends a monument to Britannia, crushing the hydra of opposition beneath his feet, and receiving a ducal coronet from Minerva. The inscription on the base glorifies the 'new Hercules'. If it was meant seriously, the naivety and extravagance of this praise sadly misfired. The suggestion of the dukedom fed opposition suspicions of Walpole's overweening ambition, and the print was re-issued with additional ironic comments on its contents and artistry. It also made a further appearance in 1741 (*BMC* 2500).

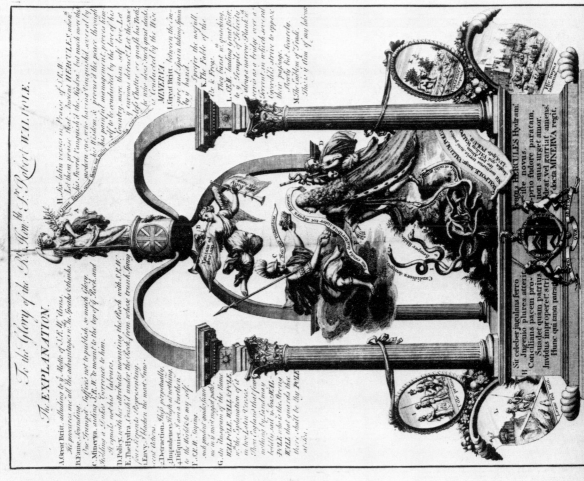

To CALEB D'ANVERS, Esq;

Mr. D'ANVERS.

To the Glory of the Rt. Hon.ble Sr Robert WALPOLE.

The EXPLANATION.

13. BMC 1841   [1730]

A companion print to *12*, plainly associating Charteris and Walpole. The parallel between the Rape-master General and the authorised ravisher of English virtue was strengthened by the assumption that Walpole had procured Charteris' pardon for reasons of his own. It seems likely that this print was produced in imitation of *12* rather than *vice-versa*.

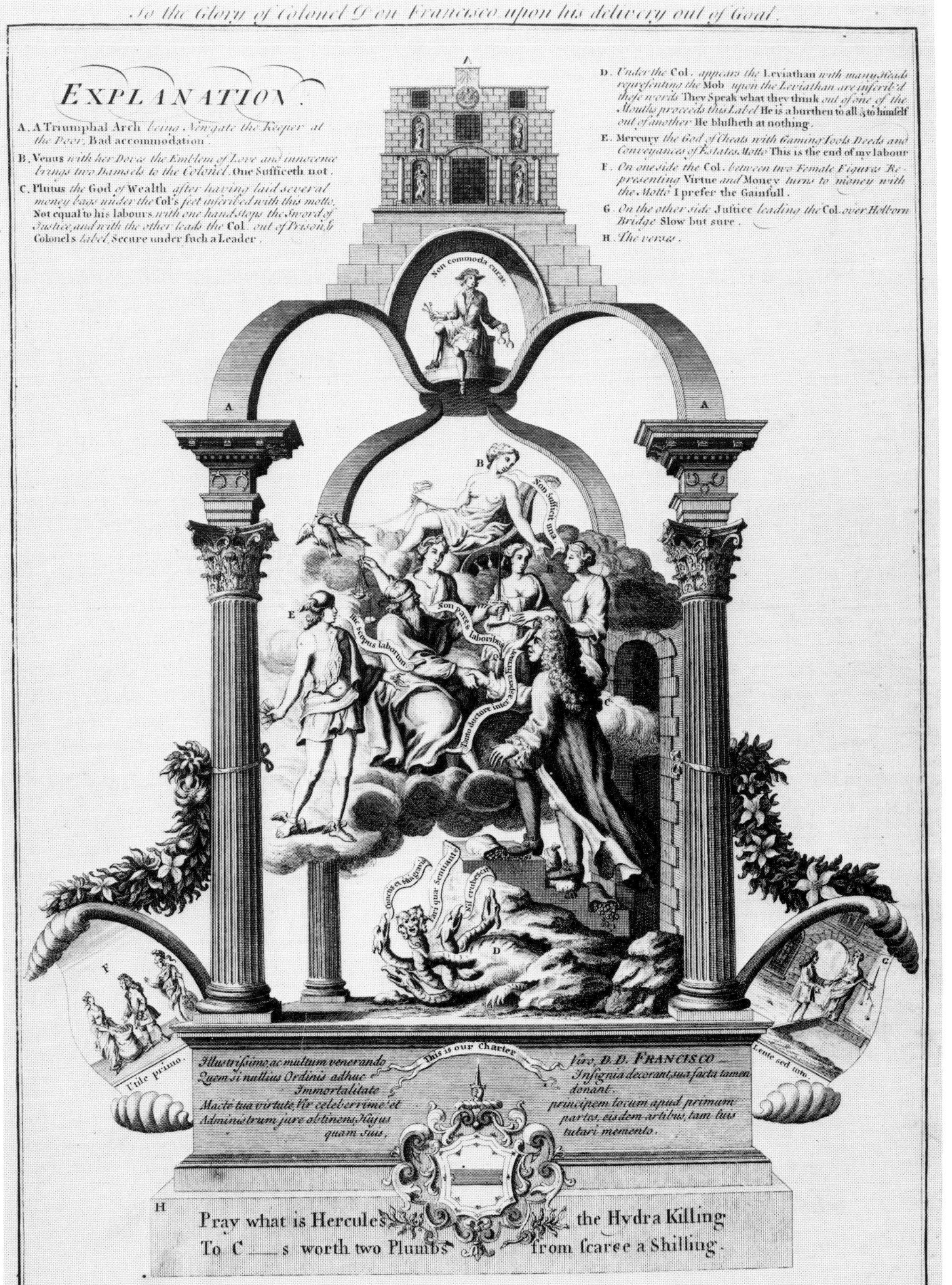
To the Glory of Colonel Don Francisco upon his delivery out of Goal.
EXPLANATION.
A. A Triumphal Arch being Newgate the Keeper at the Door, Bad accommodation.
B. Venus with her Doves the Emblem of Love and innocence brings two Damsels to the Colonel. One Sufficeth not.
C. Plutus the God of Wealth after having laid several money bags under the Col's feet inscribed with this motto, Not equal to his labours, with one hand stops the Sword of Justice, and with the other leads the Col. out of Prison, & Colonels label, Secure under such a Leader.
D. Under the Col. appears the Leviathan with many Heads representing the Mob upon the Leviathan are inscrib'd these words They Speak what they think out of one of the Mouths proceeds this Label He is a burthen to all & to himself out of another He blusheth at nothing.
E. Mercury the God of Cheats with Gaming Tools Deeds and Conveyances of Estates Motto This is the end of my labour
F. On one side the Col. between two Female Figures Representing Virtue and Money turns to money with the Motto I prefer the Gainfull.
G. On the other side Justice leading the Col. over Holborn Bridge Slow but sure.
H. The verses.
A
Non commoda curat
A
A
B
Non sufficit una
E
Non pares laboribus
C
D
Nil erubescit
This is our Charter
Illustrissimo, ac multum venerando Viro, D. D. FRANCISCO
Quem si nullius Ordinis adhuc Insignia decorant, sua facta tamen Immortalitate donant.
Macte tua virtute, Vir celeberrime et principem locum apud primum Administrum jure obtinens, Hujus partes, eisdem artibus, tam tuis quam suis, tutari memento.
F
Utile primo.
G
Lente sed tuto.
H
Pray what is Hercules the Hydra Killing
To C—s worth two Plumbs from scarce a Shilling.

1730

14.   BMC 1822   1731

One of the earliest full-scale attacks on Walpole, designed as frontispiece to a collected edition of the *Craftsman*. The case against the Robinocracy is neatly summarised. The first design has the king taking his coronation oath to preserve the liberties of his people; in the second Walpole as the 'harlequin of state' in his 'blew string' or garter sacrifices the nation to the devil; the third shows Britannia bestowing her approval on the freedom of the press; the fourth has Walpole distributing bribes to orators, lords and bishops; the fifth shows him vainly placing treaties in the scales against a complacent and triumphant Fleury; the sixth is a parody of *12*; in the final scene the editor of the *Craftsman* is encouraged by Britannia and Liberty to continue his work. The satire was hardly savage but the pamphlet which accompanied one version led to the conviction and imprisonment of its publisher for seditious libel.

ROBIN's REIGN
OR
SEVEN's THE MAIN.

Being An Explanation of
Caleb D'anvers's Seven
Egyptian Hieroglyphicks
prefixed
to the Seven Volummes
of the Craftsman.

Jacta est Alea.

Sold By the Print Sellers
of London and Westminster.
MDCCXXXI.

Price 2ˢ

Britons behold your Constitution here;
Obedience to your Laws; even Princes Swear:
Lo! high in'the sacred Volumes Play,
Source of the Subjects Right, & Monarchs sway.
Let Turks and Papists urge with equall skill,
Kings sacred Power, to Govern by their Will,
With greater Freedom, speak the British school,
By Law we're Subjects while by Law they Rule.

See here Good Folks—a Harlequin of State,
Trembling with Guilt—& yet with Pride elate.
So his great Patron—see the Villain sue,
And mark the Mischeife—Hell & he can do.
Thus Satan speaks—whole Qu'ers of W——s scat
And for your Messenger—Lo, here a Fiend:
By arts like these—you must your Foes controul,
Till Justice strike—& I receive your soul.

Hail Typographic Art:—what Blessings flow
Peace, Plenty, Justice, to thy Aid we owe:
Sacred and Civil Rights unmask'd we see,
From all the Tricks of Priests & Statesmen, free.
Their various Arts thy Noble page explains,
And Reason only unresisted Reigns.
So thou Alone, canst awe the Guilty Great,
Thy Press is the Palladium of the State.

So R——t O——'s L——s & B——y buy,
Speak then Spectator—is corruption high,
Mark well the Visage of each slavish Tool
The Blockhead Hypocrite, & saucy Fool.
Tis these Great Men, who are our Wealth away,
Borne in P——n's, but in V——s they Pray,
Like Judas thus, for Gold betray the State,
His Crimes they share, & may they share his Fate.

In this famed Ballance—mark the heavier Scale,
And see how Wisdom—does o're fraud Prevail,
Soul saving Fleury, view profoundly Wise,
By much of Thought, Depot of Power Supplies,
The Scale in steady form, his Conduct keeps,
While W——le vainly Reams of Treaties heaps,
What Briton sighs not, at the Guilty Scene,
Whence Blenheim's Robin thus reveal'd has been.

Blynded with Pride, and mad with vain Desires,
Thus to a Coronet the wretch Aspires,
Reckless of Dangers, tho' encompass'd stands,
With Insolence, his fawning slaves Command,
Thinks by his Mony, all Things may be Done,
And upwards o're the Rocks he Blunders on,
Till by one Slip from the steep Summit thrown,
His Mangled Corps, is as a Warning shown.

In Contemplation deep is D'Anvers seen,
And Tully's Eloquence directs his Pen,
Bids him his wonted Energy retain,
And still the Cause of Liberty maintain,
While Virtue thus,—since for my Sake engag'd,
Thou a just War, hast with Corruption wag'd,
Thy full Reward, in Glory then receive,
And Long as Cic'ro, let the Craftsman Live.

15. BMC 1839   [1730]

The verses tell the story of the erection of the Robinocracy after the Hanoverian Accession, of Townshend's eventual fall and of Walpole's final triumph as 'sole minister'.

The Tale of the Robbin, and the Tom-titt, Who all the Birds in the Air have bitt.

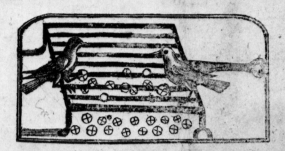

See here o'er the Grid-Iron, tho' Mony they tell.
While Peices (like Taylors,) they fink into H———h.

IN the Days of *Æsop*, as we do hear,
  All Creatures cou'd Speak, e'en Birds of the
  Who chose them a King, *de jure Divine*, (Air,
  A Term had near Spoil'd, my Political Rhyme:
  They chose them a King, as before it is said,
And flowrish'd as long, as obedience they paid;
But when a *Protector*, they chose for a King,
Dire Troubles and Wars, they with him did bring in;
Loyalists, in abundance, to Tyburn did Flock,
And the Royal King, did Submit to the Block;
The Heir they banish'd, tho' it was his right,
For which dreadfull Omens, appear'd in the Night;
Such as flashes of Fire, and Rattling the Drum,
Presageing the Plagues, And the Pest that did come;
While Angry *Jove*, from his Throne in the Sky,
His Displeasure did shew, to the Birds that did fly;
They reguardless of *Jove*, in Rebellion went on,
As they murther'd the King, so they banish'd his Son;
And thus they in Wickedness, then did proceed,
The *Vultures* instead, of the *Eagle* Succeed;
The Mirrour of Princes, and Majesty Bleed,
And Birds of Ill-Omen, alone they did feed:
For *Vultures* in Council, brought in *Cormorants*,
Whose Rav'nous Crops, swallow'd up all the *Grants*;
Such as *Robbins*, and *Rooks*, and Little *Tom-titts*,
And many such Birds, who liv'd by their Witts;
But now of my Story, of *Robbin* and *Tom*,
Who were the cheif Subjects, of this my odd Song.

The *Vulture* in Power, such Ministers chose,
Who alone for themselves, did provide meat & cloths;
Dispising such Birds, who were Honest and just,
And hateing all such, who were true to their Trust;
No Wonder such things, in those days to see,
While Banish'd remained, his good Majesty;
But to me I declare, it was a Surprize,
To find that the *Eagle*, had no better Eyes;
To think that the *Eagle*, a Guardian should make,
Tom-Titt, who all to his Coffers did take;
While the Widdow Birds, with their Young Ones
                              (Unfledg'd,
Were plundred & riffled, by Birds that were hedg'd;
To se that their Treasures, which shou'd been in store,
Was told o'er a Grid-Iorn, and dropt on the Floor;
To see the poor Birds, thus wrong'd of their Part,
Wou'd move to Compassion, the most harden'd heart;
Wherefore, indeed, it at length came about,
That the *Eagle* most Wisely, turn'd Tomy-Titt out;
O! had he turn'd *Robbin*, likewise out of Place,
It had fared much better, with the Feather'd Race
Who had felt the Effects, of that Miserly Elf,
Who had wrong'd the whole Tribe, to enrich Him-
Himself, and some few Birds, to him were a Kin, (self
To advance was the Care, of that wicked *Robbin*;
Cashiering *Robbin*, did such Chequer Work make,
What fell thro' the Grid-Iron, to himself he did take;
O! let us no more, such times see again;
But pray for the *Eagle*, with his Feathered Train.

London: Printed by K. Clifton, in Hanging-Sword Court, in Fleet Street.
Entred in the Stamp Office according to the late Act of Parliament.

16. BMC 1844   1731
    An impartial, but personalised presentation of political controversy;
    Bolingbroke (left) versus Walpole. The texts are plausible parodies of the
    arguments deployed by their respective supporters in the press. The supposed
    publishers, Figg and Sutton, were in fact popular boxers.

A clear Stage and no Favour.

CRAFTSMAN, *Saturday, December* 12, 1730.

THE PERSONS, whom you threaten, SIR, neither value your Favour, nor fear your Anger. Whenever you attempt any ACT OF POWER against any of them, you shall find that you have to do with Men, who know they have not offended the LAW; and therefore trust They have not offended the KING; who know They are safe, as long as the LAWS and LIBERTIES of their Country are so; and who are so little desirous of being safe any longer, that they would be the first to bury themselves in the Ruins of the BRITISH Constitution, if You or any M——R, as desperate as YOU, should be able to destroy it. But let us ask, on this Occasion, what YOU are, who thus presume to threaten?——Are you not ONE, whose Measure of FOLLY and INIQUITY is full; who can neither hold, nor quit his Power with Impunity; and over whose Head the long-gathering Cloud of national Vengeance is ready to burst?——Is it not Time for YOU, Sir, instead of threatening to attack OTHERS, to consider how soon you may be attacked YOURSELF?—— How many Crimes may be charged upon You and YOURS, which almost every Man can prove; and how many more are ready to start into Light, as soon as the Power, by which you now conceal them, shall determine?—— When next you meditate Revenge on your ADVERSARIES, remember this Truth. *The* LAWS *must be destroy'd, before* THEY *can suffer, or* You *escape.*

DAILY COURANT, *Monday, December* 21, 1730.

To the AUTHORS of the CRAFTSMAN.

GENTLEMEN,

THE Person whom you threaten, neither desires your Assistance, nor fears your Opposition. You have to do with a Man who knows he hath not offended the Law, who knows himself a faithful Servant to his PRINCE, and to his Country; and therefore he knows he is safe, as long as the *Laws* and *Liberties* of his Country are so: If you are come to such a Height of desperate Wickedness as to attempt to destroy your Country, because the Publick Affairs are not under your Direction, he trusts that by the Wisdom of the KING, and the Loyalty of his People, all your wicked Devices will be confounded, and all your vain Imaginations disappointed. But were it possible the vile Arts you make use of could prevail upon your Fellow Subjects to work their own Destruction, he would then think it the greatest Glory to fall by his MASTER's Side, and be buried in the Ruins of the present Establishment. Let me ask, on this Occasion, who you are, who thus presume to threaten? Are you not those whom Disappointment has fill'd with Rage, and Vanity and Ambition depriv'd of Reason? Is it not time for you, instead of threatning to attack others, to reflect upon your own Guilt, who have made it your Business, by scandalous Parallels, and malicious Insinuations, to render his Majesty's Person and Government odious and contemptible to his People? This is a Crime, which every Man who reads your Papers can witness you are justly charged with. When next you meditate Mischief against the Person whom you injure because you envy, and hate because you have injur'd, remember this Truth, While the Laws have their due Force, and a JUST PRINCE fills the Throne, you cannot ruin an innocent Man, and cloath yourselves with his Spoils.

LONDON: Printed for Messieurs FIGG and SUTTON. MDCCXXXI.   [Price 6 *d.*]

17. BMC 1868   [1731]
The duel, which arose from a pamphleteering controversy and was fought on 26 January 1731, resulted only in a slight wound for Hervey. In the print Walpole is made the villain, wishing ill not merely to his enemy Pulteney but to his friend Hervey: 'Let them cut one anothers Throats'.

Duel between Lord Hervey and the Hon.ble William Pulteney.

A CONSEQUENCE of the MOTION

See Pl — men, where ends all your Scribling | The Smost fluid F—d may fight most hourly | Th: Fox in smiles his Spleen do's smother
P— t— y and B—gh jobbing | The honest Y—k—ne t—ks more smartly | And gladly i'd give in all this father
To hurth the Toils of R—   Needle &c. | Took care his J— is streight should part ye   Bristle &c. | The D— done to feed the Other.   Brittle &c.

Sold by T. Kirhon on Ludhull, London.   Brittle &c.

18. BMC 1870   [July 1731]
   A simple representation of the viciousness of George II's court. Walpole is the thriving courtier, Pulteney (recently humiliated by his removal from the Privy Council) the slighted courtier, Hervey, ironically, the honest courtier. The print originally appeared as frontispiece to a satirical pamphlet on Pulteney's disgrace.

THREE COURTIERS. 1731.

The Honest Courtier

The Thriving Courtier

The Slighted Courtier

19. BMC 1871 [1731] George Bickham
A contemptuous gibe at 'Orator' Henley. Frustrated in his pursuit of ecclesiastical preferment, Henley had in 1726 established an 'oratory' open to all-comers. His unorthodox theology and theatrical rhetoric attracted much attention and controversy. He was also a strong supporter of Walpole; the print includes several references to the ministerial journal of which he was author, the *Hyp-Doctor*.

THE
ORATORY.

Inveniam Viam aut faciam

Colley Cibber

In præsens ut prosequar

Hyp doctor k egan 9th Jan 1731

1731

An extempore Epigram made at ye Oratory.

O! Orator; with brazen face and lungs;
Whose jargon's form'd of ten unlearned Tongues;
Why stand'st thou there a whole long hour harranguing,
When half the time fits better Men for hanging?

Grub Street journal May 13. 1731.

See Broo Dict. Henley. Nichols Hogarth b.

Geo B. & A. jun. Copper Somchers Strode Invent Sculp

MODESTY.

MERIT.

20.   BMC 1898   26 October 1732

Published in the *Grub-Street Journal* to illustrate the working conditions of printers' 'devils', this emblematic satire was accompanied by an account of the great variety of publications being produced by an over-worked press. Shown are the better-known political journals as well as such items as medical treatises.

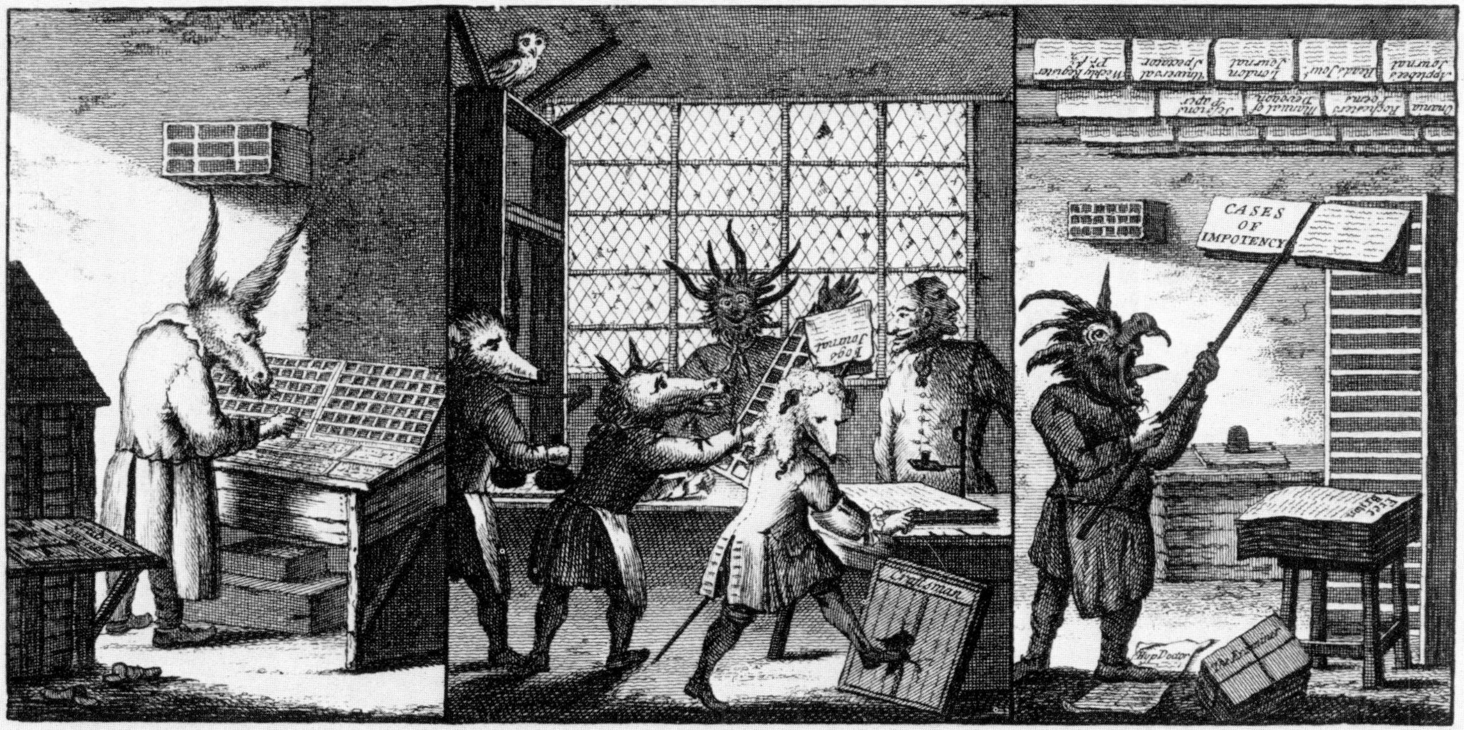
CASES
OF
IMPOTENCY

21. BMC 1904   [1732]
   Frontispiece to an account of the fraudulent practices of the South Sea
   Company. Under the terms of the Treaty of Utrecht the Company had limited
   rights of trade with Spain's American colonies. By various means, including the
   use of Britain's West Indian islands and the attendance on the 'annual ship' of
   smaller craft, the Company in fact carried far larger quantities of goods than
   was permitted. The profit of these transactions was reaped not by the
   Company's proprietors but by the directors and their agents. Walpole plausibly
   argued that it was impossible to remedy the proprietors' grievance without
   publicly admitting that the British were violating international law. Nonetheless
   the resulting action led to a parliamentary enquiry, culminating in 1733 in a
   damaging, though inconclusive, crisis in the House of Lords.

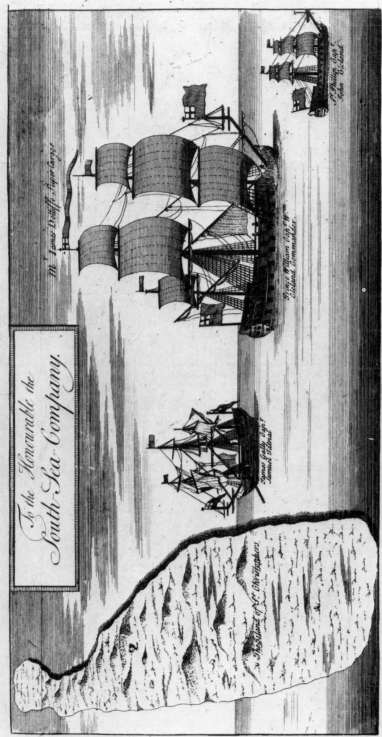

To the Honourable the
South-Sea-Company.

Ph.² James Dolliff. Super-Cargo.

Prince William Cap.ᵗ W.ᵐ
Cleland Commander.

James Gally. Cap.ᵗ
Samuel Girard.

the Island of St. Christophers.

J.ᵗ Phillip. Cap.ᵗ
John Cleland.

In Miniature behold your South Sea Fleet ——— As if the Crafty Scheme at first was laid.
Bound from St. Kitts to carry on the Cheat ——— To turn to Private Use our Foreign Trade.

22. BMC 1918 [March–April 1733]
The excise crisis in its early stages. Walpole is borne along by a brutal grenadier and a cowed British lion wearing wooden shoes. Troops of the standing army cheer him on and the weather vane over Westminster, where his proposals initially achieved substantial majorities, points significantly in his direction.

EXCISE IN TRIUMPH

Sr.R.Walpole. Dejected Trade hangs down its drooping Head,
While Standing Armies daring Colours spread;
By these encourag'd, on the Bark strides;
Excise in Triumph, and like Bacchus rides:
They clap French Shoes upon the British Beast.
Still to enslave, and make us more distrest
Oh! —— ceace such wicked Arts pursuing
Or you your self may be Excis'd for shoeing.

1. Trade.
2. Excise on a Hogshead
3. Tobacco
3. Standing Army.

4. A Tame Lyon.
5. A Hall.
6. A Pallace.

Excise Bill. 1733.

23. BMC 1936   [March–April 1733]
This popular ballad with woodcut caused the government to order the arrest of hawkers selling it. It depicts Walpole being pulled along by the many-headed monster excise, which regurgitates money into his lap.

BRITANNIA Excisa:

Britain Excis'd.

FOLK S talk of Supplies
  To be rais'd by *Excise*,
Old *CALEB* is bloodily nettl'd;
  Sure *B*----- has more Sense,
  Than to levy new Pence,
Or Troops, when his Peace is quite settl'd.
  Horse, Foot, and Dragoons,
  Battalions, Platoons,
Excise, Wooden Shoes, and no Jury;
  Then Taxes increasing,
  While Traffick is ceasing,
Would put all the Land in a Fury.

II.
  From whence I conclude,
  This is wrong understood,
From his Cradle *B*----- hated Oppression,
  And our King Good and Great
  Would have us All eat,
Then dread not, good People, next Session.
  Horse, Foot, and Dragoons,
  Battalions, Platoons, &c.

III.
  See this Dragon, E X C I S E,
  Has Ten Thousand Eyes,
And Five Thousand Mouths to devour us,
  A Sting and sharp Claws,
  With wide-gaping Jaws,
And a Belly as big as a Store-house.
  Horse, Foot, and Dragoons,
  Battalions, Platoons, &c.

IV.
  This Monster, Plague rot him!
  The Pope first begot him,
From *Rome* to King *Lewis* he went;
  From a *Papist* so true,
  What Good can ensue?
No Wonder he'll make you keep *Lent.*
  Horse, Foot, and Dragoons,
  Battalions, Platoons, &c.

V.
  From *France* he flew over,
  And landed at *Dover,*
To swill down your Ale and your Beer;
  Now he swears he can't dine,
  Without Sugar and Wine;
Thus he'll plunder you Year after Year.
  Horse, Foot, and Dragoons,
  Battalions, Platoons, &c.

VI.
  Grant these, and the Glutton
  Will roar out for Mutton,
Your Beef, Bread and Bacon to boot;
  Your Goose, Pig, and Pullet,
  He'll thrust down his Gullet,
Whilst the Labourer munches a Root.
  Horse, Foot, and Dragoons,
  Battalions, Platoons, &c.

VII.
  Besides, 'tis decreed,
C The Monster must feed,

24. BMC 1920   [March–April 1733]
The true beneficiaries of the excise scheme are revealed. The arms display a version of *22*, a grenadier and a gin-seller with false measure. On the right is a tobacconist, on the left a cheating ale-house keeper. A short measure flagon surmounts the arms. The message was deliberately misleading. Fraudulent traders had nothing to gain from the supervision of excise officials, as their furious opposition to the scheme confirms.

The PUBLICAN'S COAT of ARMS.
Explain'd and Figur'd

25. BMC 1922   [March–April 1733]
    Walpole and his parliamentary opponents. This frontispiece to a mock sermon ironically extolling the merits of the excise scheme, shows Walpole leaving the House of Commons and declaring 'It must and shall pass'. The M.P.s represented are those who had taken a lead in opposing the excise.

A. St. Alban's. B. Newton. C. Heddon. D. Somerset. E. Kent. F. Middlesex.
G. London. H. Hert S: — I. Heddon. K. Abingdon L. Aldborough. M. Beverly.
G. London.

Frontispiece to Winers Excise Sermon 14 Mar: 1733.

26. BMC 1921   [March–April 1733]
    Resistance to the excise scheme is celebrated. When Walpole formally introduced his project for an excise on tobacco on 14 March he obtained an initial majority of 265 to 204. Here the 204 are congratulated, with pride of place going to the two London M.P.s named on the maypole, Micajah Perry and Sir John Barnard. Justice weighs Magna Carta in her scales against wooden shoes and manacles. On the right trade and liberty rejoice. Fame and plenty hover about. It is possible that this print was produced when Walpole had abandoned his scheme in mid-April, but more likely that it followed hard on the division of 14 March and was meant to incite further opposition.

THE NOBLE STAND: Or the GLORIOUS CCXIIII.

Sacred to their Immortal Honour down to the latest Posterity.

Arise Britannia, Joyfull now-arise!
And to th' pleasing prospect turn thy eye!
See, Justice triumph's! Victory how compleat?
Oppression grovelling lies beneath her feet!
Her Scales aloft, She bears: One of them, Chains;
And Wooden Shoes, and Gauging Rules contains:

England's Great Charter in the other view;
London's Petition, Two hundred and twice two ∗
How richly weighty these; while these appear
Like empty bubbles mounting in the air —
Two hogsheads, on the right, stand, fill'd by full;
This, with Tobacco; that with Wine supply'd:

On these fair Liberty, Divinely bright,
And Trade, with fixed look, you eye delight.
Plenty defends, and with a gracious smile ∗
How e'er down her besiege on thy happy Isle.
Fame spread wide the Joyfull news reports:
The Offspring heart's join in rural sports:
A Cosy Maypole, with Tobacco bound,
And the thrice fruit, they raise and dance around.

∗ The number of the Members who oppos'd the Excise Bill.

Perry & Bernard City Members upon the Bill.

April 1733

Price 6^d.

27. BMC 1926   [April 1733]

The defeat of the excise approaches. The campaign against the scheme culminated in the petition of the City of London, drawn up on 9 April (top scene) and presented to the Commons on the 10th. Walpole succeeded in having it rejected by a narrow margin but then announced his withdrawal of the excise proposals. He had made this decision the evening before, but the timing of his announcement, which was calculated to make it appear that he was not giving way to pressure from the City, had precisely the contrary effect. In the bottom scene the monster excise is slain, to universal joy. The print may possibly have been published as part of Lord Mayor Barber's unsuccessful campaign for election as one of the City's M.P.s a year later.

Monday April 9, at a Meeting of the Common-Council of this City, the Right Hon:^ble the LORD MAYOR was pleas'd to introduce the Business of the Day in the following Words.

GENTLEMEN, There is a Bill depending in the House of Commons, (a Copy of w:^ch I have procur'd) laying an Inland Duty on Tobacco; w:^ch Duty, it is universally agreed, will prove extreemly detrimental to the Trade & Commerce of this great City, as well as to That of the whole Nation. And as the High Station, w:^ch I have the Honour to be in, obliges me to be watchfull over every Thing that may affect the Interest of my Fellow-Citizens, I should think Myself wanting in my Duty, if I neglected to call you together on this Extraordinary Occasion, that you might have an Opportunity to deliberate on an Affair of such Importance, wherein our Liberty & our Property are so essentially concerned.— And the Bill being read, the following Petition was agreed to unanimously. Vٟz.

To the Honourable the Commons of Great Britain in Parliament assembled.

The Humble Petition of ŷ Lord Mayor, Aldermen, & Commons of this City of LONDON in Common Council Assembled.

SHEWETH,

That your Petitioners observe in the Votes of this Honourable House, that a Bill has been brought in, pursuant to the Resolutions of the Sixteenth Day of March, for Repealing several Subsidies & an Impost now payable on Tobacco of the British Plantations, & for granting an Inland Duty in Lieu thereof.

That they presume therefore in all Humility, by a respectful Application to this House, to express, as they have already done, in some Measure, by their Instructions to their Members, the Universal Sense of the City of LONDON, concerning any further Extension of the Laws of Excise.

That ŷ Burthen of Taxes already imposed on every Branch of Trade, however chearfully born, is severely felt; but ŷ ŷ Petitioners apprehend this Burthen will grow too heavy to be born, if it be increas'd by such vexatious & oppressive Methods of levying & collecting ŷ Duties, as they are assur'd by malencholy Experience, ŷ Nature of all Excises must necessarily produce.

That the Merchants, Tradesmen & Manufacturers of this Kingdom have supported themselves under ŷ Pressure of ŷ Excise Laws now in Force, by ŷ comfortable & reasonable Expectation, ŷ Laws which nothing but publick Necessity could be a Motive to enact, would be repealed in Favour of ŷ Trade of ŷ Nation, & of ŷ Liberty of ŷ Subject, whenever ŷ Motive should be removed, as ŷ Petitioners presume it effectually is, by an undisturb'd Tranquillity at Home, & a general Peace so firmly establish'd Abroad.

That if this Expectation be entirely taken away; if ŷ Excise Laws, instead of being repeal'd, are extended to other Species of Merchandize, not yet Excised, & a Door open'd for extending them to all, ŷ Petitioners cannot, in Justice to themselves, to the Merchants, Tradesmen & Manufacturers of ŷ whole Kingdom, & to the general Interest of their Country, conceal their Apprehension, that ŷ most fatal Blow, w:^ch ever was given, will be given on this Occasion, to the Trade & Navigation of GREAT BRITAIN, that great Spring, from w:^ch the Wealth & Prosperity of ŷ Publick flows, will be obstructed, ŷ Mercantile Part of ŷ Nation will become not only less able to Trade to Advantage, but unwilling to Trade at all; for no Person who can enjoy all ŷ Privileges of a British Subject out of Trade, even with a small Fortune, will voluntarily renounce some of the most valuable of those Privileges, by subjecting himself to the Laws of Excise.

That if Petitioners are able to shew, ŷ these their Apprehensions are founded both in Experience & Reason, & therefore your Petit:^rs most humbly pray, That this Hon:^ble House will be pleas'd to hear them by their Council against the said Bill.

April. 1733.

28. BMC 1937   [April 1733]
The triumphant sequel to *23*. The first scene is a poor copy of the earlier print, the second shows Walpole coming to grief, and the third depicts the mob burning ministerial journals before the statue of Charles I at Charing Cross.

Britannia Excisa.

CHARLES. I.

Excise Congress.

BRITANNIA EXCISA. Part II.

29. BMC 1925   [1733]
     The comparison with Wolsey is spelled out on the medallion and reinforced by
     the presence of a church in the background. On the left appears a glimpse of the
     monster excise. The design of which this is a part, meant for a fan, is produced
     in full by H. M. Atherton, *Political Prints in the Age of Hogarth*, Plate 13.

WOLSEY AND HIS SUCCESSOR HERE IN ONE BEHOLD, BOTH SERV'D THEIR MASTERS BOTH THEIR COUNTRY SOLD.

Liberty and Property

No Excise Wood has Carry Enrich the Devil

R. H....n

30. BMC 1927   [June 1733]
    The defeat of the excise is celebrated and Walpole burnt in effigy. The scene
    takes place in front of the Royal Exchange, symbol of British trade. In the
    Commons Walpole had unwisely used the expression 'sturdy beggars' to
    describe those fraudulent merchants who had a vested interest in the excise. The
    phrase was thenceforward turned against him and used ironically of all
    businessmen.

1733

THE LONDON MERCHANTS TRIUMPHANT
(or Sturdy Beggars are Brave Fellows)
being a Sketch of the Rejoyceings in the Citty &c. Occation'd by the Excize Bill being Postpon'd.

Exciseman & Walpole burnt in Effigy April. 12. 1733. See Smollett. Bk. II. ch. V. §. 6. Perry, Barnard, Pulteney & Wyndham oppose the Excise Bill. Exciseman

Long, Long live the Glorious Two hundred and four:
And may we Such Senators have evermore.
Whom. Places nor Pensions, will ever persuade
To give up our Juries, and Fetter our Trade;
Who Steadily Zealous, are always prepard
To Maintain English Rights, & our Liberties guar
But a Curse on the Slaves, who Excises insist on,
May they daily be horse-ponded, pelted and pist on.

Ap. 1733.

31. BMC 1940   [1733]
     This frontispiece to an 'excise opera' entitled *The State Juggler* rejoices in the failure of Walpole's scheme. The British lion and Britannia enjoy their pipes while a grenadier and exciseman mournfully look on.

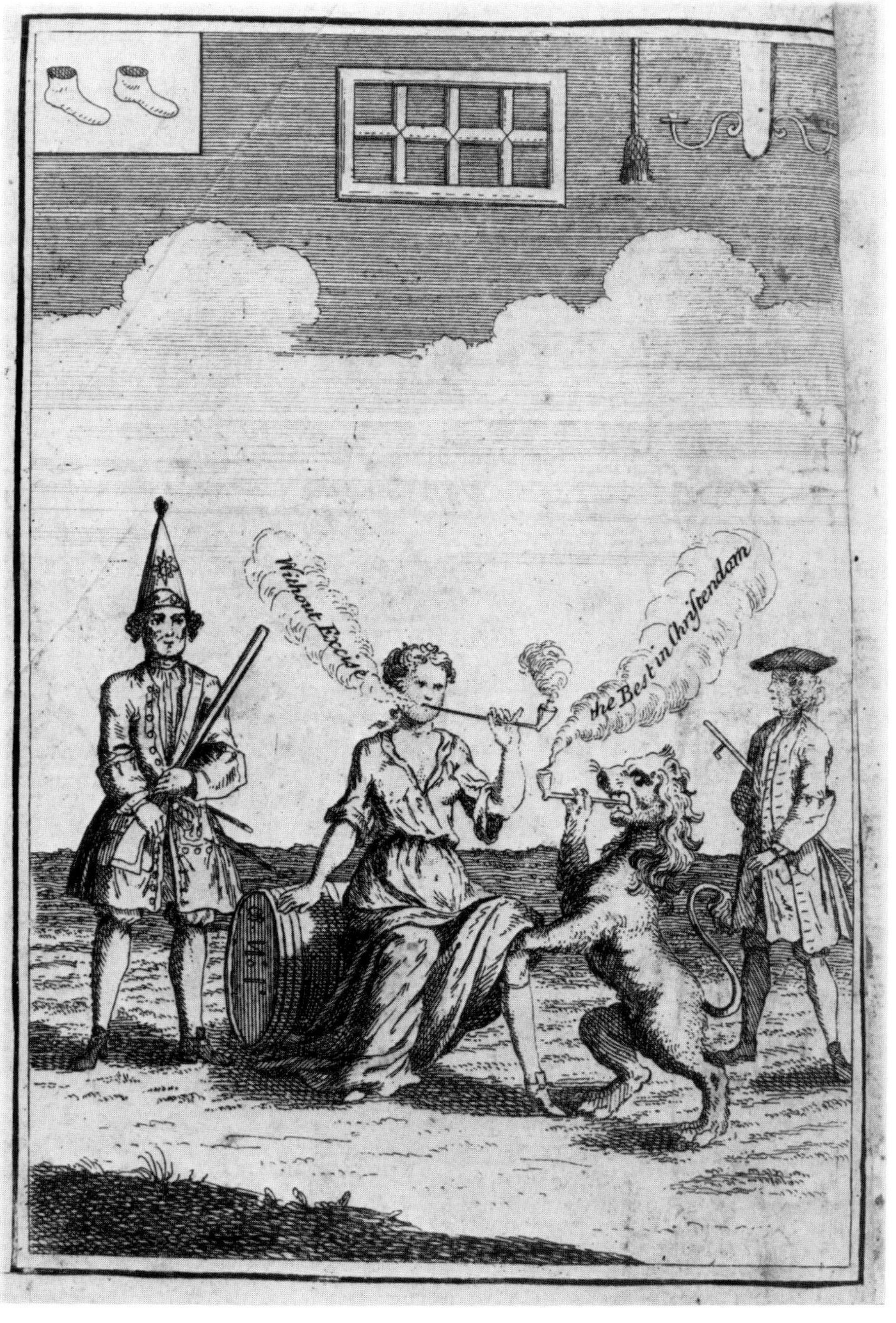

Without Excise
the Best in Christendom

32. BMC 1931   [August 1733]

This ironic comment on Walpole's reception in his home county in the summer of 1733, was issued with a ballad entitled *The Quack Triumphant, or, The N–r—ch Cavalcade*. Walpole's triumphant entry into Norwich was part of a carefully prepared campaign for the next general election and an attempt to obscure the damaging effects of the excise crisis. Walpole is here pictured as a quack doctor, Sir Sidrophel, with his brother Horace as his wretched servant Whaccum. These characters were drawn from Samuel Butler's mock heroic poem *Hudibras* in which Sidrophel, a charlatan and conjuror, was first consulted and then thrashed by the hero Hudibras.

Behold the great Sir Sidrophel   Who does such cures no man can tell
Quack Whaccum to the croud   As is by all allow'd
                                    All Sickness flies at his Approach
                                    Here take his Pills — You'll keep your lane

33. BMC 1924   [October 1733]
     In St. Paul's on 7 October 1733 David Scurlock preached the Christian duty of
     obedience to government and denounced the City tradesmen who had
     petitioned against the excise scheme. The sermon was said to have provoked
     outrage among his audience and also met with a hostile reception in the press,
     which attacked Scurlock as a defender of passive obedience and imitator of the
     notorious Dr. Sacheverell.

A Whip for the Horse a Bridle for the Ass,
and a Rod for the Fools Back. Prov: XXVI. 3.

For that worthy Man. P. & Proving irrefragably. I. D. o. P. O. a. N. R. In Defence of Passive Obedience & Non Resista

34. BMC 1939 [1733]
     The anticipated execution of Walpole. His headless body is dragged along, followed by a troop of mourning excisemen, balances in hand. Two historical parallels are suggested: Sejanus the corrupt tool of a vicious emperor, and the De Witts, the brothers lynched by the Dutch mob in 1672 for crimes against the Republic. The women in the background are bent on mutilating and burning a corpse which may be either Walpole's or, to sustain the analogy with the De Witts, that of his brother Horace.

The Downfall of SEJANUS, &c.

Since Bribes in modren Days so much prevail,
And Votes have daily been Expos'd to Sale;
Since Courtly Roosters finds his Cause decline,
And Gold's the Refuge of his last Design;
Tis Time brave Britons to Defend your Right,
Nor tamely sink beneath th' oppressive Weight.
Be yours the glorious Task of just Defence,
To save your Country, and espouse your Prince,
To crush Ambition in its wild Career,
And thunder Vengeance in the Statesmans Ear:
Sever the free-born Native from the Slave,
Degrade the Unworthy, and exalt the Brave
Then wisely on; nor let th' Infection spread
The Mischief ripens and demands your Aid:

Explode th' Ungen'rous Schemists who'd betray
The Nations Weal and give her Right away
Exert, once more, your Breast in Freedoms Cause
(For virtuous Caution claims no mean Applause)
Freedom! of all Prerogatives the Cheif
Confer'd by Nature to distinguish Life
Honours first Child, and Object of our Choice,
Nor aw'd by Faction, nor deter'd by Vice;
Bold as a Lion which supports her Cause,
And wars Revenge where Force invades her laws
Spurns the weak Statesmans faithless glittring Power
And spite of Gold, derides his baffled Power

1733

35. BMC 1928   [1734]

Further exultation at the failure of the excise. In the first scene Britannia refuses Walpole's offer of the excise; Walpole wears a Jacobite kilt. Behind Britannia the papacy awaits an advantage; below her the continental victims of Walpole's foreign policy look ineffectually on. In the second scene, Walpole vainly attempts to sacrifice Magna Carta. He is encouraged by Satan and Cardinal Fleury, while French merchant ships prosper at the expense of their British rivals. The surrounding medals include an axe tied in the 'blew ribbon' and Walpole on the gallows. Above the hanging scene are monsters representing the court journalists Walsingham (William Arnall) and Osborne (James Pitt).

The Scheme Disappointed
A Fruitless Sacrifice
D.M.
EXCISÆ GNATÆ
CARISSIMÆ ROB
PATER
M.P.
WALSINGHAM
OSBORN'S Works
Fig 1 BRITTAIN intent on Magna Charta, repulsing Fig 2 R. Walpole Offering her the Excise Scheme. Fig 3. SCOTLAND. Fig 4. The Empire directing Fig 5. A naked Boy with a pointless Sword (the Princes of the Empire) to look up to Brittain. Fig 6. A Bull dog licking and overturning an Imperial Crown the Map of Naples & Sicily lying before Fig 7 Rome ready to seize Brittain if she accepts the Scheme.
The Medals
Fig 1 An Ax ty'd up in a Ribbon. (2) Nobles bowing to one who throws Money in their hats. (3) The same led to execution, the People rejoicing. (4.5) Two rapacious Harpies. (6) A Cock pecking out an Eagles eyes. (7) Acteon torn by his own dogs. (8) A Lyon hung up by the heels struggling to get loose. (9) A Serpent twisted round a Throne. (10) An Inscription by the mournfull Father of the Excise, to his deceas'd Child. (11) A Lady in Chains dejected & her Spear broken. (12) A Ship in a tempest her Masts broke & Flags drooping. (13) A Judge holding a Ballance, his Foot in one of the Scales. (14) Punch at a Table writing dispatches. (15.16) Two Mysterious Sphinxes (17.18) Two Monsters vomiting Gold into a Vase, which is swallowed by (19.20) Two Ostriches, an Animal whose Stomach digests Metal. (21) A Groupe of hang'd Figures some mark'd with Roses & some with Thistles.
Fig 1 Walpole The Sacrificer on his knees pushing a Torch to Magna Charta &c. but the fire not kindl'd, the Sacrifice directed to, Fig 2 The Devil holding out with one hand the Excise Scheme, the other holds a Rope & Fig 3. A Cardinal Fleury with one hand holding out a bag to the Sacrificer, with the other grasping at a Globe in the Clouds. Fig. 4. The Altar a Pile of Books founded on a heap of Gold with proper Inscriptions Fig 5 The Statue of Brittain on a Column held by an Almighty hand. Fig 6. The British Fleet in Port. Fig. 7. The French Fleet under Sail.
Ap. 1733.

36. BMC 2026   [February 1734]
In this frontispiece to a ballad entitled *The Court Monkies*, Walpole (seated) and his friend Sir William Yonge make wooden shoes for the subjects of George II. The apes have a double significance, as the ballad reveals. Employed in making fetters they are partly designed to reinforce the despotic implication of the first scene, partly to represent Walpole's journalistic hacks. Pope to whom the ballad was dedicated, was often, as a result of his deformity, shown ape-like, and the image was sometimes extended to his Grub-Street rivals and enemies.

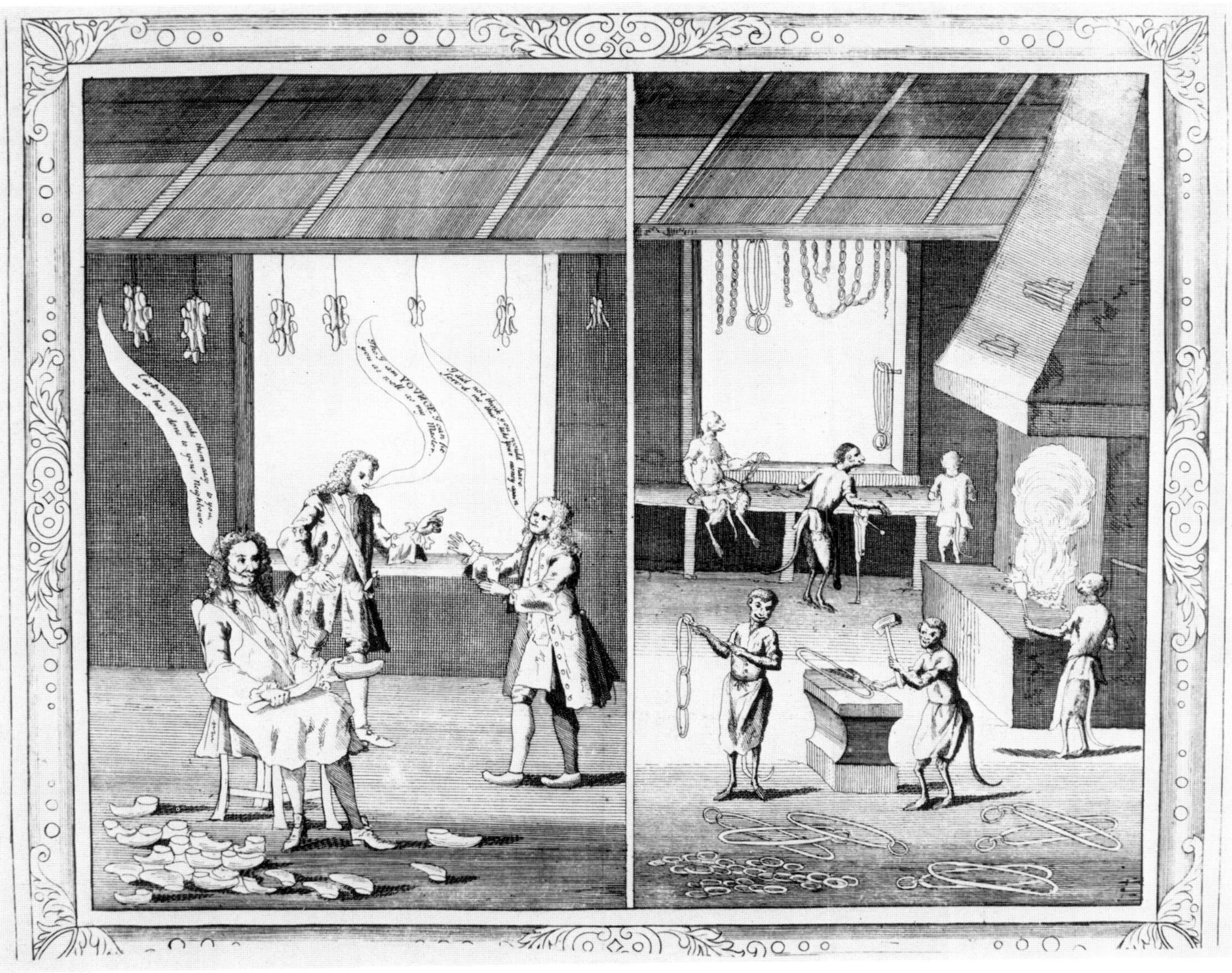
Custom will make them easy to you, as it has done to your Neighbours.
Tho' I am YOUNGE I can fit you as well as my Master.
I did not think you would have serv'd me thus: take your money again

37. BMC 2017   [1734]

A reasonably impartial depiction of the county election for Kent in the general election of 1734. On the hustings the freeholders await their turn to vote. In the foreground, left, the supporters of the country party candidates, Sir Edward Dering and Lord Vane, cry 'No Excise'. Against them are matched the followers of the court candidates, the Earl of Middlesex and Sir George Oxenden, who shout 'King and Country' and 'Protestant Interest'. The outcome was a victory for the opposition and a clear indication of the unpopularity of the excise with electors. Walpole remained in power after the general election thanks only to his control of the smaller, more corrupt constituencies.

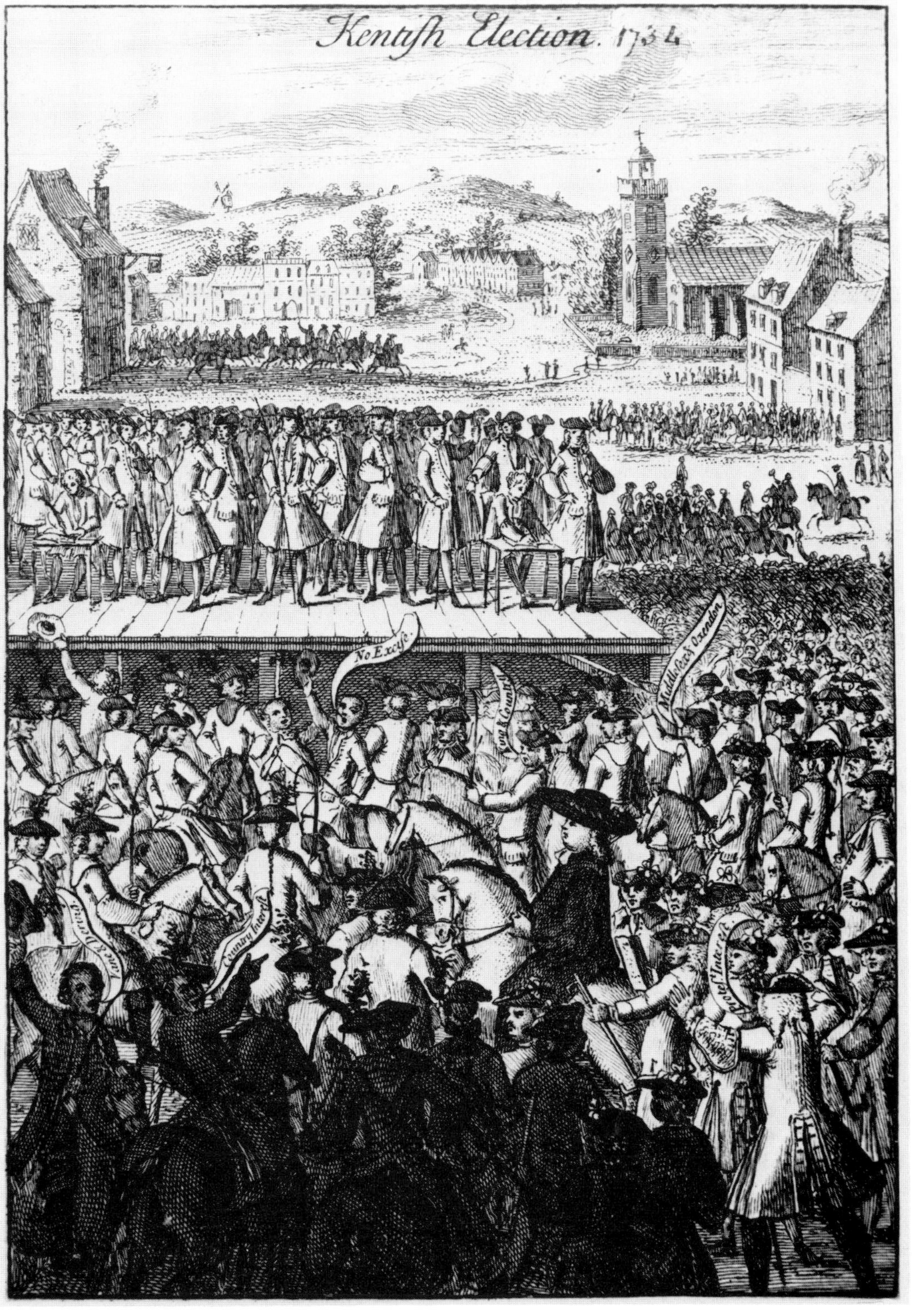
Kentish Election. 1734
No Excise
King & Country
Middlesex & Oxenden
Vane & Dering
Country Interest

38. BMC 2030   [June 1734]
    The candidates arrive, corrupt the voters, and are then chaired in triumph in
    this illustration to a play published after the general election of 1734 *(The
    Humours of a Country Election)*. The constituency is plainly a decayed
    borough, and there is no competition.

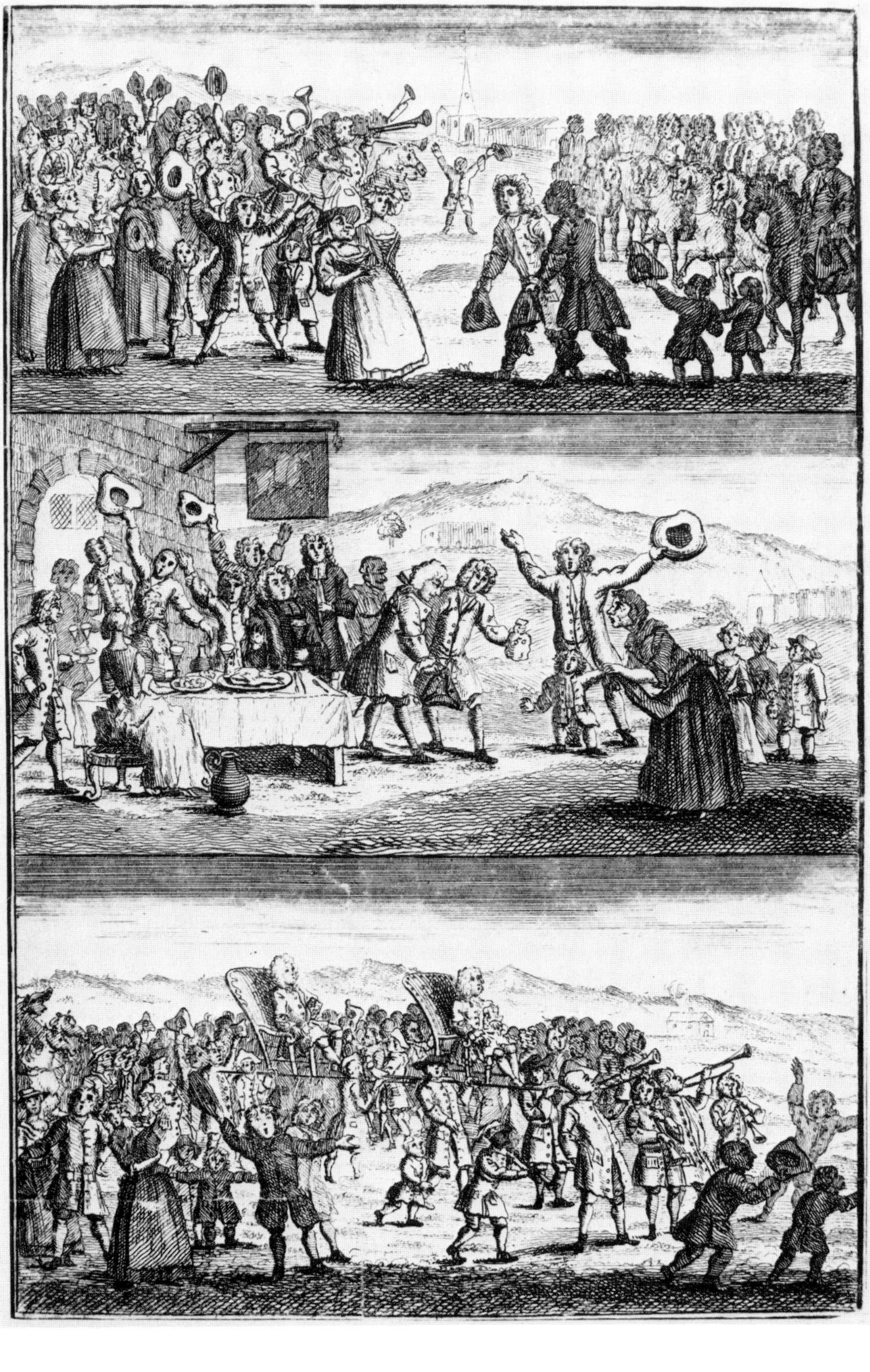

39. BMC 2025   [1734]

An emblematic attack on the corruption of the Robinocracy, published with a ballad, entitled *A Collection of State Flowers*. On the left is the dominating presence of the sunflower Walpole. In the foreground there flourish other corrupt plants: five pinks or Lords of the Treasury, and the sixteen thistles or representative peers of Scotland (in 1734–5 an unsuccessful protest was made against the government's control of the Scottish elections to the House of Lords). In the background, right, lies an uprooted English rose. In the centre a healthy plant, the Charitable Corporation, showers money designed for the worthy poor; but it is about to be hacked down by its trustees. Two of the latter, Sir Robert Sutton and Sir Archibald Grant, had been expelled from the Commons in 1732 for their venality, notwithstanding vigorous attempts by Walpole to protect them.

Two Treasury Pinks

Ready upon occasion

40. BMC 2140   [18 January 1735]
     The opening session of the new Parliament elected in 1734 is presented as a
     farce, with the Walpole brothers as the leading actors.

BY PERMISSION.

This is to give Notice to all Gentlemen and Ladies, & others

That.

At the OPERA House in the HAYMARKET

This present *Evening will be presented the comicall and.

diverting Humours of.

PUNCH.

And on Thursday next by the Norfolk Company of artificiall

Commedians at ROBINS great Theatricall Booth PALACE

YARD will be presented a comical and diverting PLAY of Seven

ACTS call'd COURT and COUNTRY in which will be

revived ÿ: entertaining Scene of

The Blundering Brothers

with the Cheats of

RABBI ROBBIN

Prime Minister to King SOLOMON. the whole concluding with

a grand MASQUE call'd the DOWNFALL of SEJANUS. or the

STATESMAN OVERTHROWN

with Axes, Halters Gibbetts & other Decorations proper for the Play.

to begin exactly at Twelve o' Clock.

N.B. Those are a new sett of Puppets as big as the Life ÿ chief part of which

have been brought up from all parts of ÿ Country at a very great Espence

VIVANT REX ET REGINA

* Jan: 18: 1734 i.e. 1735   Jan. 1735

41. BMC 2268   [c. 1735]
The prostitutes and physicians of state administer their panacea of gold to the expiring patient. Walpole, seated, directs the operation. On the wall the engravings include the works of Hogarth.

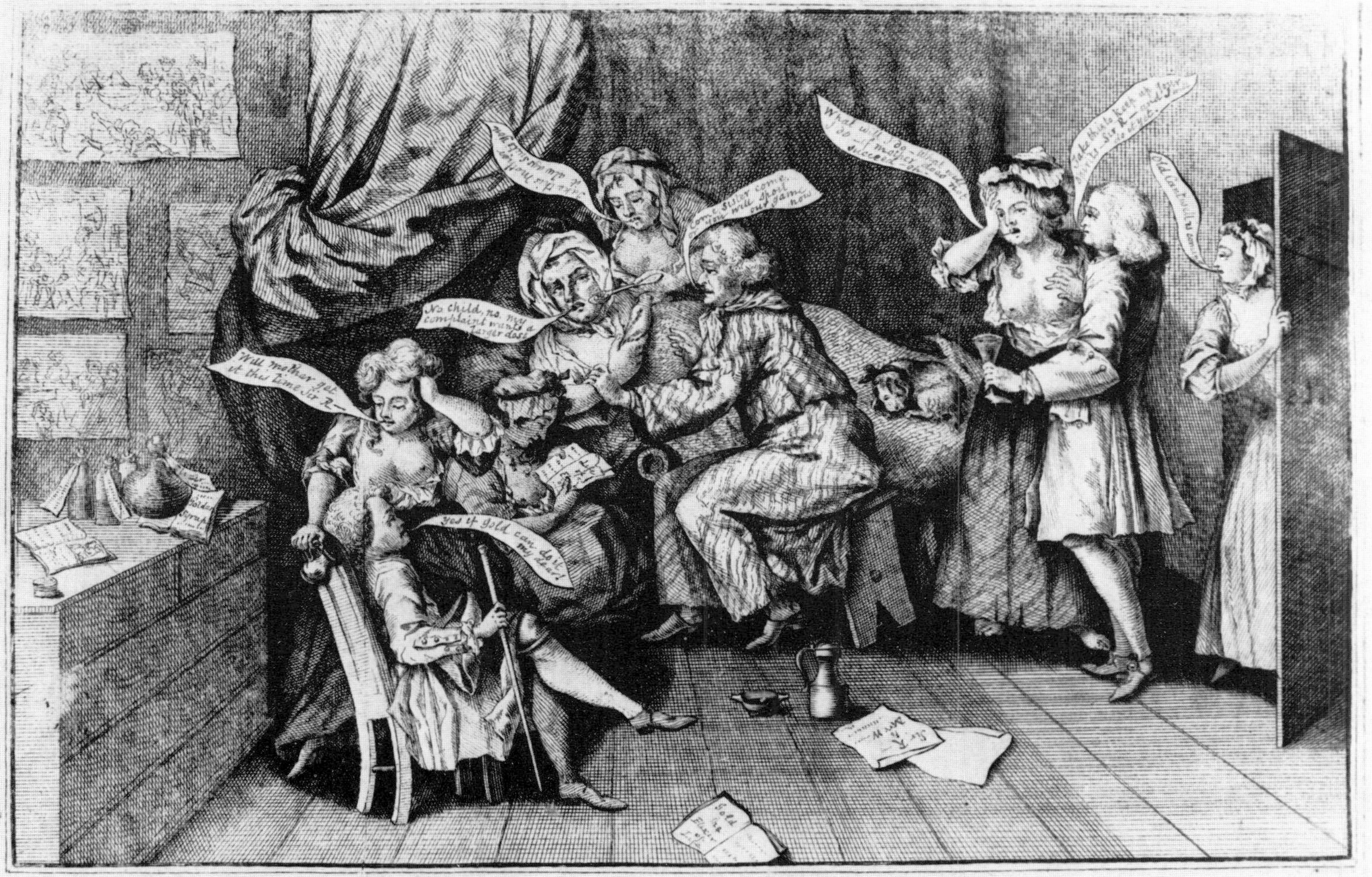

Will mother get it this time Sir R—
No child, no, my complaint wants a larger dose
Yes if gold can do it my dear!
Old Cantwell is coming

42. BMC 1938   [1735]

A satire inspired by, but much inferior to, Hogarth's *Rake's Progress*. Walpole is shown first at Oxford (in fact, unlike the Rake he was at Cambridge) where fortune encourages him, then at his election for Parliament, thirdly in prison after his expulsion by the Commons for alleged corruption, and fourthly drawing comfort from the accession of George I. Three scenes display his varying fortunes during the Stanhope era: his unsuccessful attempt to oust Stanhope, his languishing in opposition, his lucky elevation as a result of Stanhope's death. Finally he is shown taking his last and supposedly fatal step in the excise crisis.

R—B—N's PROGRESS in Eight Scenes:
From His first Coming up from Oxford to London to his present Situation.

Scene I.

Scene II

Scene III

Scene IV.

Scene VIII

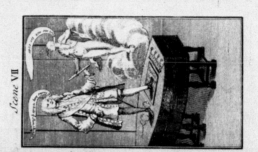

Scene VII

Scene VI

Scene V

43. BMC 2149   1735

An attack on Walpole's 'Pope', Gibson. The skimmington was the traditional means of humiliating a hen-pecked husband, who was led in procession by his wife to the accompaniment of popular jeering and ribaldry. Here the church is shown leading the state. The central figure is Gibson himself who drags his *Codex Juris Ecclesiastici Anglicani* of 1713 behind him. Preceded by Jesuitical clergy, whose banners bear the names of eminent divines, his eye is on the 'prospect' of the Archbishop of Canterbury. On the right the populace protest against his supposedly High Church views. In particular Gibson opposed a Mortmain Bill which reduced the privileges of ecclesiastical corporations and charities, and bills which would have repealed the Test and Corporation Acts and relieved the Quakers' grievances concerning tithes. His campaign, in addition to incensing dissenters and latitudinarians, was disastrous for his relations with his old ally Walpole, and in truth ruined his chances of obtaining Canterbury.

The HIERARCHICAL SKIMINGTON: Or a Representation of the Ambitious and Arbitrary Views of a Party.

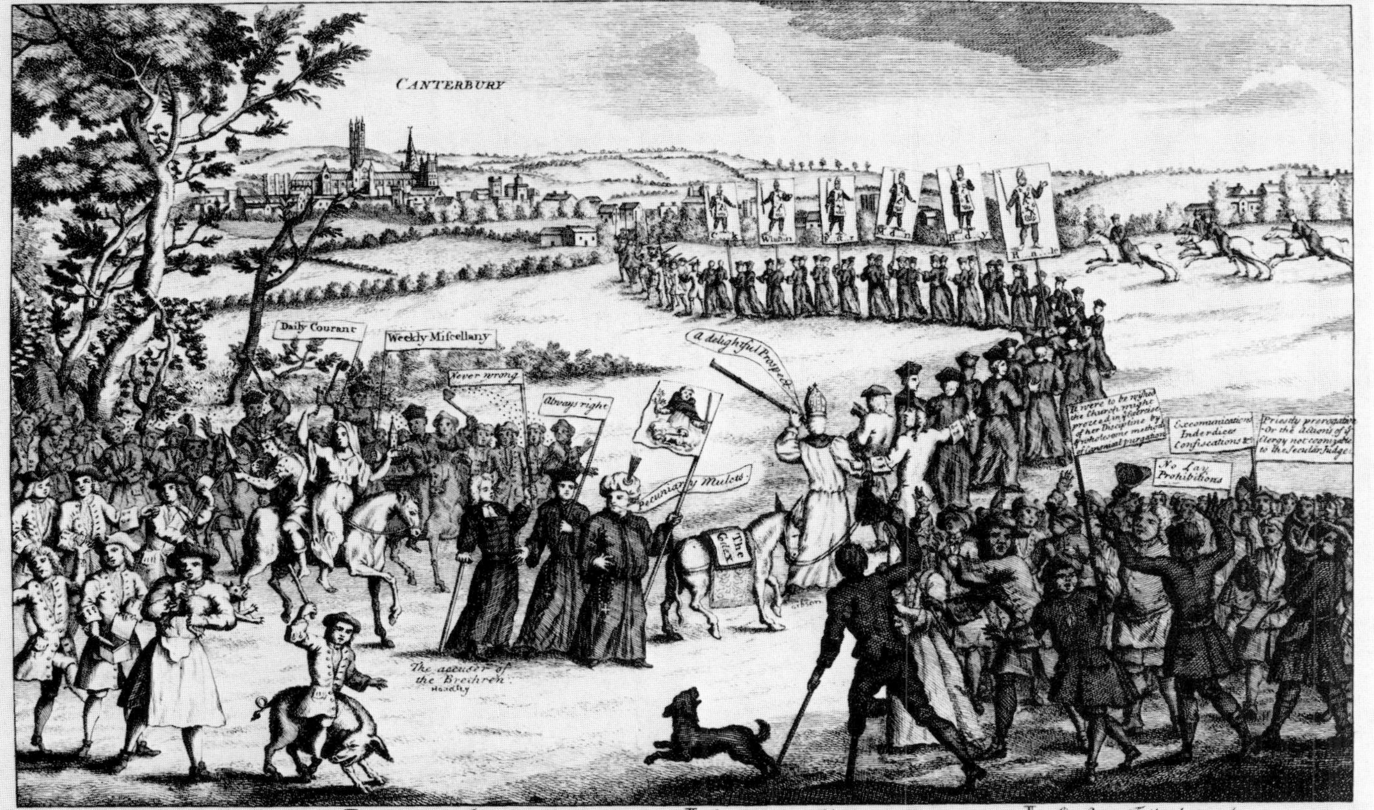

CANTERBURY
Daily Courant
Weekly Miscellany
Never wrong
Always right
A delightful Prospect
Pecuniary Mulcts
The accuser of the Brethren
Excommunications Interdicts Confiscations &c
No Lay Prohibitions

This Emblematic Piece before ye
Displays the Priesthood in their Glory,
And at one View discovers what
The H...h Ch....h Brethren would be at.
First, in procession march along
Of Jesuits a numerous throng,
Bearing aloft, that all may see,
The Sons of Schism in Effigie.

Behind, with Telescope in hand
A Reverend Brother makes a Stand
To view a distant City, which
In little time he hopes to reach;
But lo! his friend, in Sudden fright
Pulls him, and pointing to the right
Bawls out Come on! Step forward or ye
Will find yon Jockies there before ye:

Slow moves an Ass along the Road,
His Back supports a heavy load.
But what is he with Turbant drest?
An English or a Turkish Priest?
Behind, two others march along,
This always right, that never wrong
' Next them, behold, the Church triumphant
' Bestrides her beast, and on the Rump on't

' Sits face to Tail & bum to bum
' The State by pious frauds o'ercome,
' Arm'd with a Spindle and a Distaff,
' Which, as he rides, She makes him twist off;
' And, when he loiters o'er her Shoulder
' Chastises Reformade Soldier.
Behind, before and round about,
Attend the drunken Rabble Rout

1735

44. BMC 2280   [1736]
   The campaign against Gibson continued in a straightforward but highly
   misleading comparison with Archbishop Laud.

THE PARALLEL:

Or, Laud &c C-d-x compared. Being a true Picture of those celebrated High Priests, shewing the great Resemblance between them, both in principles and practice.

Britons beware! —— Mark them which cause divisions and offences —— they serve not our Lord Jesus Christ, but their own belly. —— Thro' Covetousness shall they with feigned words, make Merchandize of you. Rom: 16: ver: 17:18. —— 2 Peter 2. ver: 3. Put them in mind that as they are English men and Protestants, they ought to be Subject to Potentates and Powers, and to obey the Civil Magistrate.

45. BMC 2269   [c. 1736]
    Ecclesiastical corruption in the Walpole era. Archbishop Wake follows his son-
    in-law John Lynch, whose many preferments were supposed to derive from his
    manipulation of Wake during the latter's last years. An obsequious cleric does
    homage to the ass.

Dr Lynch, Son in law to ABp Wake.

Lynch. Dean Canterbury

Publish'd According to Act of Parliament
L.d Hardwick.

An ASS loaded w.th PREFERMENTS.

In Days of Old the Churchman that wou'd Shine.
If not Apostle, was at least Divine:
A Supple Conscience now & Front of Brass,
For highest Honours fits the heaviest Ass.

Ten thousand Souls in one Squab Doctor's care.
Give him no Pain, Sinecure's are not dear.
Good antient Pastors us'd to feed and keep.
Enough't for ous, that they can Shear, their Sheep.

46. BMC 2326   [January] 1738
A sarcastic comment on George II's survival of a storm which threatened to wreck the royal yacht when he set out from Hanover to England in December 1736. One of the clouds is imitating the king's well-known habit of kicking his hat.

ÆNEAS in a STORM.

She *that th' indignous Winds & Deep deform* ~
Smiles on y' Tumult, & enjoys y' Storm ~

1737

Published pursuant to an Act of Parliament 1737

Price 6.d

Tanta hæc Mulier potuit Suadere Malorum

47. BMC 2329   [October 1737]

One of the earliest appearances of the theme of Spanish depradations which was to cause Walpole so many difficulties. Here the source of Britain's humiliations at the hands of Spanish-American coastguards is traced back to the failure of Admiral Hosier's expedition of 1726. In the text it is argued that Portobello had offered an easy target for the navy. The *London Evening Post* was one of Walpole's most vociferous enemies in the press and played a major part in the opposition campaign against his foreign policy.

To the Author of the London Evening-Post.

Oct. 16, 1737.

SIR,

READING your Evening Paper of the 6th Instant, wherein you have related a most flagrant Fact of Piracy now among many others lately committed on our Shipping by the *Spanish* Nation, I find you say the Opinions concerning these perpetual Depredations of the *Spaniards* on us are various; and then you seemingly give it as your own, that this proceeds from the beating and destroying their Fleet by Admiral *Byng* in the Year 1718: This possibly, as you observe, may stick in their unforgiving Stomachs; but leaving the Dead to rest in Peace, and Actions such as these to be buried with them, it is my Opinion, that if at all we merit Condemnation, our Sins will be found to proceed more from *Omission* than *Commission*, and we may date our Losses from that ever-memorable Expedition of *Hosier's* Squadron (too unhappy Admiral) in the *West Indies*. I will not deny but before that Time our Reputation declined, and our Merchants, by many Losses, found the sad Effects too truly verify'd; these were the Beginnings but of future Evils, the mortal Blow was given by our own Shipping, and the extraordinary Behaviour of that *unfortunate* but *brave Navy* on the Coast of *Spanish Porto Bello*, first opened the Eyes of that haughty People, the Charm at once dissolv'd, the Spell vanish'd, and old Terrors, caus'd by former *British* Squadrons, now like a past Enchantment ended, left every *little Fellow* of that Nation at Liberty to *insult us* with Impunity.

To explain a little these Matters; your Readers must know that the Galleons are Merchant Ships of *Spain*, who at certain Times sail under Convoy of two or more Men of War, loaded with a valuable Cargo from *Europe* for *Porto Bello*, when the great Merchants of *Peru*, with their Treasures of Gold and Silver, meet them; and thus, by the Confluence of those two grand Commerces of *Peru* and *Europe*, an inestimable Wealth of many Millions is deposited in that defenceless Place: A fine Harbour, indeed, as the Name signifies, and guarded sufficiently from every other Accident save an Enemy only. The Place itself is without Walls, its whole Strength consisting in three ancient Castles or Towers, built on Eminencies, and which at the Times of Bows and Arrows might be held of some Importance: But weak as these were by Art and Nature, they were much more so by Neglect; for not long before the Arrival of *Hosier's* Squadron myself saw the principal Cannon of the strongest Fort, some mounted only on Logs of Wood, and others half buried under the Earth; Garrison they had none, or any other Force that I could ever see in the whole Place, (and I have been conversant amongst them) except about 30 or 40 ragged Fellows, to whom a Party of our Train'd-Bands would seem an Host of *Alexanders*. This was the Strength of *Porto-Bello*, when at that Time the Galleons, under the Convoy of two Ships of War, all of them unrigg'd, unloaded and disarm'd, lay sleeping at their Anchors, little dreaming of an Enemy so near them, the whole Treasure of *Peru*, consisting of 20 Millions in Gold and Silver, all the Loading of the Galleons, in Goods of equal Value, in careless Security then lodg'd on Shore in Wooden Ware-houses, when early at Dawn of Day one Morning was seen the *British* Squadron, drawn up in Line of Battle, their Sails all full, and steering with a steady Gale right favourable for them directly for the Harbour's Mouth. 'Tis not to be conceiv'd the Consternation caus'd by this unexpected Appearance, and the Terror, when at their nearer Approach the once dreaded *British* Colours were distinguished; no Thoughts nor Time for Resistance then, but every Man contriving how, at the Expence of his Treasure, he might save his Life: What added still to their Despair was, that not one Mule could be found in *Porto-Bello*, all being at that Instant actually at *Panama*, so that the very Means, if willing, of saving any thing, was taken from them. This was the State of Things on *Hosier's* Approach, Heaven and Earth seem'd to conspire to make every Accident answer to his utmost Wishes; Conquest courted his Acceptance with the richest Prize that ever fell to Man; the Occasion now presented (never to come again) of being easy Master of *Peru's* Wealth without Bloodshed; when at the Instant it was expected he should make his Entrance to take Possession, he suddenly sheer'd off and stood for the *Bastimentos*; the dismal Catastrophe of that, the finest Squadron, both for Commanders, Men, and Ships, these Seas yet ever saw, is but too well known during their Stay in that accursed Place; grating Remembrance this to every Englishman, a Scene too truly tragical to be forgot: *Hosier* himself was brave even to Rashness; from whence then could proceed an Infatuation such as this? I have heard (but God knows how true) that the Tenour of his Instructions were only to *persuade* the *Spaniards* to deliver themselves and Wealth up to him, and so this mighty Squadron to carry Terror in Appearance only: However that be, this we all know, his Ships lay rotting in the *Bastimentos*, his Men all sick and dying, himself and most of his Commanders dead with Vexation and Despair; the Island of *Jamaica* was drain'd afterwards of its Sailors for his Recruits, and hardly sufficient this to navigate at last his Worm-eaten Ships from that inhospitable Shoar. Myself have often heard the Governor of *Porto Bello* say, that he has sent Boats by Night to the *Bastimentos*, and they have pass'd through the whole Squadron without being once haled or questioned by them, hardly a Soul thro' Death or Sickness, appearing upon the Decks; 'till at last, this Act so oft repeated, embolden'd the *Spaniards* to that degree, that I knew the Man among them who proposed to the Governor, with the Sloops of *Porto Bello*, furnish'd as he should chuse, to bring the *British* Squadron captive into that Harbour. Thus by degrees had their first Terrors vanished, and Insolence succeeded in its place, and it was by this means these People, unknowing of the Tenour of that unhappy Admiral's Instructions, attribured at last to Fear, what proceeded only from a too fatal Necessity: From hence they build their Presumption; they who before hardly dar'd to look towards that Sea while a *British* Squadron sail'd on it, now scower the same Ocean from End to End, making shameful Prize of all Ships they can overcome thereon, and by our *tame* and *peaceful* Sufferance take it for granted that we have not the *Courage* to resent it.

48. BMC 2327 [March] 1737

A savage satire on the court of George II. Walpole, with his magician's wand, presides over the ceremony. Queen Caroline injects the magic potion needed to calm the spirits of her husband while Horace Walpole with his scales (signifying his mediatory skills) looks on. Courtiers worship in attitudes of abject slavery. The rump was a favourite image in connection with George II. The Rump-Steak Club had been formed by peers who had had the royal back turned upon them at court, and rump worship was much discussed in the press in 1737. A lengthy description of the ceremony was published in *Common Sense* for 19 March 1737.

THE FESTIVAL OF THE GOLDEN RUMP.
Rumpatur, quisquis Rumpitur invidiâ.

UNA EURUSQ.
NOTUSQ: RUUNT
CREBERQ. PROCELLIS
AFRICUS

Design'd by the Author of Common Sense.

Publish'd according to Act of Parliament 1737.   Price 1s.

49. BMC 2346   [1737]

An oblique reference to the quarrel between George II and Frederick, Prince of Wales. Attention is directed to the picture displaying the expulsion of Adam and Eve from Eden. The Princess of Wales, in the final stages of her first pregnancy, was removed by her husband from the supervision of the queen at Hampton Court, to St. James's. The king reacted to this insult by requiring the offenders to find their own residence. The rift considerably strengthened the opposition and was to have the most damaging consequences for Walpole, who had no option but to side with the court.

J. Gubernator Inv.

Ham. Princeps Scul.

Et Nugis addere Pondus. Hor.

50.   BMC 2333   10 October 1737   Charles Mosley
The first of an important series of prints attacking Walpole's foreign policy.
While the French fox takes the lead following its successes in the War of the
Polish Succession, pulling the Spanish wolf and Russian bear in its wake, the
Turkish elephant follows but has slipped its tie to France. Holland on a boar
remains at the starting post. Sardinia in a chariot has still to arrive at it. Corsica
is unseated by its rebellious mount, while Austria on its imperial eagle has yet to
join the race. Most important are the suggestions of British feebleness. The lion
is held back before the starting post, a bulldog broods sullenly below the
umpires' box, and Walpole, on horseback, offers to sell Gibraltar, Minorca, or
Georgia to the Pretender, who is betting on Cardinal Fleury's French fox. In the
centre foreground a raree-showman displays the portrait of a woman (more
likely than feats of a war to attract the interest of the King of England) and on
his back reveals an image of the Pretender. In the background, below a glimpse
of St. Paul's, a Spanish fleet prepares to take Gibraltar, while the British fleet
remains inactive.

THE EUROPEAN RACE

Heat 1ᵗ ANNO DOM. MDCCXXVII

*France, Spain, Ruſſia, Turky, Germany, Italy
Quaſi Obedient Servant* — *An Englishman.*

*Humbly inscrib'd to ye Politicians of Great Britain,
Holland and Corſica, by their*

51. BMC 2331   [1738]
A critique of the government of George II. In the background Blenheim Palace reminds the viewer of the martial triumphs of Marlborough, contrasting with Walpole's inglorious appeasement of the Bourbon powers. Queen Anne, heroine of the Tories and embodiment of the ancient Elizabethan virtues, appears with an account of her achievements, designed to emphasise the corrupt, wasteful and unpatriotic conduct of a Hanoverian king.

The following Character
of her late Majesty
QUEEN ANNE
was Written by her Grace
Sarah Dutchess
of Marlborough
& is cut Round this Pedestal

Erected at BLENHEIM.

Queen ANNE was very Graceful & Majestic in her Person. Religious without Affectation; she always meant well. She had no false Ambition, which appear'd, by her never complaining at King William's being preferr'd to the Crown before her, when it was taken from the King her father, for following such Counsels & pursuing such Measures as rendered the Revolution necessary; it was Her greatest Affliction to act against Him even for Security; her Journey to Nottingham was never concerted, but occasioned by the great Consternation she was under at the King's sudden return from Salisbury. She always paid the greatest Respect to King William & Queen Mary; never insisted upon any one Circumstance of Grandeur More than what was establish'd in her Family by King Charles II, though after the Revolution She was Presumptive Heir to the Crown, & after ye Death of her Sister was in the Place of Prince of Wales. Upon her Accession to the Throne, the Civil-list was not increased. The late Earl of Godolphin Lord High Treasurer of England has often said, that from Accidents in the Customs, & Lenity in the Collection it did not arise one Year with another to more than Five Hundred Thousand Pounds a Year. She had

no Vanity in Her Expences, nor bought any one Jewel in the whole Time of her Reign. She paid out of her Civil-list many Pensions granted in former Reigns which have since been thrown upon the Publick. when a War was necessary to secure Europe against the Power of France, She contributed in one Year towards the War, out of her Civil-list, one Hundred Thousand Pounds, in Ease of her Subjects; She granted the Revenue arising from the first fruits, to augment the Provision of the poorer Clergy. She never refus'd her private Charity to proper Objects. Till a Few Years before her Death, she never had but Twenty Thousand Pounds a Year for her Privy Purse; at the latter End of her Reign it did not exceed Twenty Six Thousand Pounds a Year; which was much to her Honour, because it is Subject to no Accounts. And as it will appear by the Records in the Exchequer, that in Nine Years, she spent only Thirty two Thousand & Fifty Pounds including ye Coronation Expence. She was extremly well bred, treated her chief Ladies & Servants as if they had been Her Equals; her behaviour to all that approached Her was decent & full of Dignity, and shew'd Condescention, without Art or Meanness: all this I know to be true. SARAH MARLBOROUGH 1738

52. BMC 2336   1738

The *Craftsman*'s portrayal of Walpole's system. Time breaks its chain and
Britannia proffers an olive branch while Nicholas Amhurst, as 'Caleb
D'Anvers', editor of the *Craftsman*, displays his painting. Walpole is shown
beneath a gallows from which hangs an earl's coronet. He directs the
destruction of his country by corruption and taxation. Trade is ruined, and the
Admiralty fails to provide protection against Spanish interference.

To all *True Lovers of Liberty*; *Merchants*, *Landholders*, *Freeholders*, and other *Electors* to *parliament*, to *Returning Officers*, & to all *Clear-Sighted Honest Men*; this piece is *Humbly Inscribed*

by their *Most Obedient Servant*
Dry Bob.

Amhurst, alias Caleb D'Anvers, Editor of The Craftsman.
Publish according to Act of Parliament 1738

1738

53. BMC 2347   27 October 1738   George Bickham
   Walpole's complacency in the growing crisis over Spanish depredations in Latin America. He pats the lion on its head while its talons are removed by Spain, whose daughter exposes her breasts to the leering Walpole. As a sop to increasing public alarm about Spain's activities against British merchantmen, Walpole had despatched a squadron under Admiral Haddock to the Mediterranean; it was widely believed that he was on the point of giving in to Spain's demand for Haddock's recall.

THE
Lyon in Love.
OR THE
POLITICAL FARMER.
An Æsopian Tale,
Applicable to the present Times.

A Lyon, once to Love inclin'd,   Those Grinders may perhaps offend her:—
Thus to a Farmer break his Mind:—   Let them be Drawn, & pare your Nails,
Your Daughter, Sir,— then fetch'd a Sigh—   The Bargain's struck,— Hang him if fails.
Give me Your Daughter, or I die.—   O'erjoy'd the Amorous Fool complies,
Hob, stood aghast,— then made a Pause.—   And, like a whining Coxcomb cries,
But weighing well his length of Claws,   Polly's the Only Thing I prize.
And the huge Fangs between his Jaws,   The Job perform'd, & all things safe.—
Consented to his mad Petition;   Hob, & all round him grin, and laugh.—
But notwithstanding on Condition.   Fearless, grow monstrously uncivil,
Poll, Sir, you know, is young & tender:—   And Send him packing to the D—l.

THE
APPLICATION.

Call Home Your Fleet cries Artful SPAIN,—
And BRITAIN shall no more complain.—
But should we be such Fools—What then?
We should be Slaves,— be drub'd again.—

27 Octr. 1738

Walpole.

Britons Rebellion.

All Safe

27 d Octr. 1738 Publish'd According to Late Act. Price 6d

Reluctance of Walpole to engage in War. See Smollett. Bk. II. ch. VI. & v. VI.

54. BMC 2415   26 November 1738   Charles Mosley

A sequel to *50*. Fleury still leads the race, but he is now followed by the King of Corsica who has quelled his rebellious subjects and threatens France. Spain stumbles after, while Turkey, though gravely injured as a result of the year's military campaign, has overtaken Russia. Austria has now succeeded in joining the race but makes little progress, and the Dutch remain at the starting post, clogged like some of the other competitors by a French fleur de lys. A British cannon has finally made its appearance but its muzzle is stopped and the lions pulling it are restrained. Don Carlos, King of the Two Sicilies, makes difficult progress with his Italian chariot. Among the figures in the foreground a butcher stands ready to release the British bulldog. In the background is the familiar criticism of British pusillanimity in the West Indies.

THE EUROPEAN RACE

Heat II.ᵈ Anno Dom. MDCCXXXVIII.

Inscrib'd to the Politicians of the Universe

By their Humble Serv:ᵗ An Englishman.

has commandments for this is the whole Duty of Man

Let us hear the conclusion of the whole matter. Fear God and keep

Ecclesiastes the 12ᵗ Verse the 13ᵗ

55. BMC 2348   19 December 1738   Bispham Dickinson?
    George II with his mistress Madame Wallmoden, later Countess of Yarmouth.
    A portrait of the dead Queen Caroline is on the far wall, and on the left-hand
    wall is a dress of mourning for her. The popularity of this print is attested by the
    fact that it was still selling well enough to be involved in a government
    prosecution of obscene prints in 1749.

SOLOMON in his Glory.

Come let us take our Fill of Love untill the Morning let us Solace our selves
with Love; For the Good Man is not at Home, He is gone a Long Journey,
He hath taken A Bag of Money with him & will come home at the Day Appointed.

Queen Caroline died 1 Dec. 1737   Proverbs 7. 18. 19. 20.
Publish'd According to Act of Parliment Dec: 19 1738   19. Dec. 1738

56. BMC 2350   1738   George Bickham?
(derived from Breugel's 'The Rich Kitchen')
A further attack on the government's attitude towards negotiations with Spain. Walpole pushes away the protesting Captain Jenkins (the latter carrying his severed ear), while France bribes his mistress and a courtier ejects a remonstrating British merchant. A glimpse of a naval vessel overwhelming a Spanish galleon suggests the alternative to Walpole's feeble foreign policy.

IN PLACE. 1737.

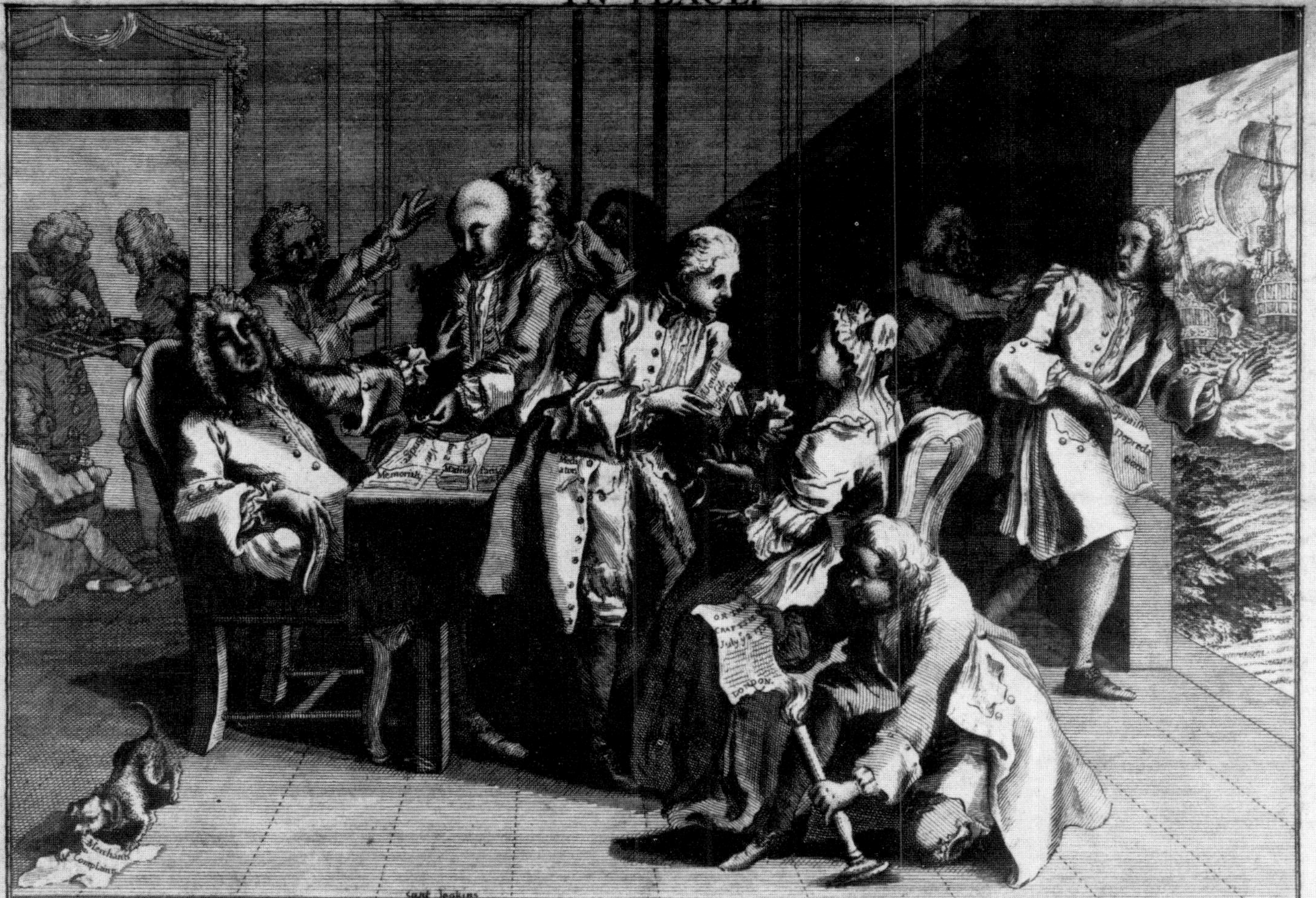
Merchants Complaints
Memorials
Capt Jenkins

Smoll. Bk 11. ch. VI. & VI. — Walpole

The Great man easy sits in Borrow'd State,
The millions suffer by the Yoke of State. —
Values not Widows Cries or Orphans Tears, —
Nor Depredations or the loss of Ears.
Capt Jenkins ears cut off by Spaniards.

The Injur'd Merchant calmly brings his Case,
And craves Redress from him who is in Place. —
But to compleat his loss sustain'd before —
Is by a Court Tool push'd out o'th' Door. —
See Smollet. Bk 11. ch. VI. & 17.

While Monsieur makes a candid application —
And hopes they will accept his Mediation. — France sent Ambass. to mediate. Sept. 1739.
But Britons boldly shew Imperious Spain, —
What tis to rouze the Masters of the Main. —

1738.

Publish'd & Inv. by a Friend to y Court
According to y late Act 1738. Price 6 Pence.

57. BMC 2353   [1738]

A blatant piece of warmongering, designed as frontispiece to *The Voice of Liberty; or, a British Philippic*. British seamen lie in a Spanish prison in the West Indies. The shades of great admirals of the past, Cavendish, Raleigh and Blake, appear overhead, while Britannia responds to their call and British warships rally to the defence of trade.

And dare they, dare the vanquish'd sons of Spain
Enslave a Briton *?*

58. BMC 2355   [1738]
More war-hysteria. Walpole compels the British lion to trail along behind a Spanish ploughman who has harnessed English merchant-seamen to his yoke. Jenkins is shown losing his ear and a warship of the royal navy fails to resist a Spanish attack.

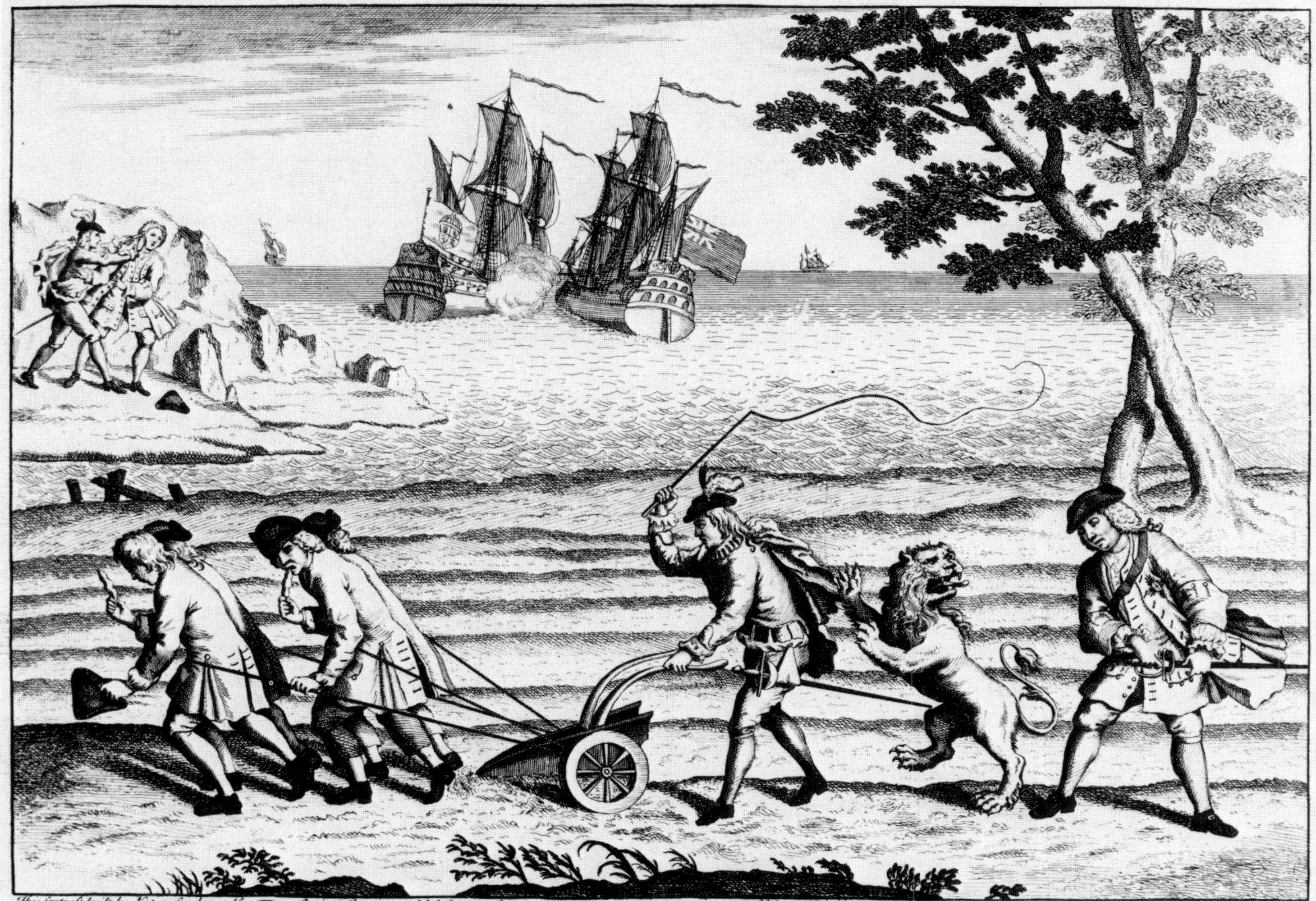

SLAVERY.

This fortress built by Nature for her self,
Against infection, and the hand of War;
This happy breed of men this little world;
This precious stone set in the silver sea,
Which serves it in the office of a Wall,
Or as a moat defensive to a House,

Against the envy of less happy Lands;
This nurse, this teeming womb of royal Kings,
Fear'd for their Breed, & famous for their birth,
Renown'd for their deeds, as far from home,
For christian service and true chivalry,
As is the sepulchre in stubborn Jewry

Of the worlds ransom, blessed Mary's son
This land of such dear souls, this dear dear land,
Dear for her reputation through the World,
Is now leas'd out, (I die pronouncing it)
Like to a tenement, or pelting farm,
England bound in with the triumphant sea,

Whose rocky shore beats back the envious siege
Of watry Neptune, is bound in with shame,
With inky blots, & rotten parchment bonds.

Shakespears K. Richard 2

Capt. Jenkins ear cut off by Spaniards. See Smoll Hist

To the Worthy and most Injur'd MERCHANTS of Great Britain. This Print is most humbly Inscrib'd

Publish'd according to a late Act.

1738

59. BMC 2150 [1739]

Walpole at the zenith of his power, attended by fortune with her wheel and a Jew with his money bag. Below him rages the great battle of court and country. On the left liberty despairs as the courtiers receive gold from Walpole's angel of corruption. On the right opposition raise their swords in impotent defiance. The print appeared as the frontispiece to Bolingbroke's *Dissertation upon Parties*, which had originally been issued in instalments in the *Craftsman* and was now published in its fifth collected edition.

Dissertation upon parties. Letters to Caleb D'Anvers

1739.

Sr Robt. Walpole & his
Opposition Trentothee
t out to a Publication

60. BMC 2352   26 January 1739

Criticism of Walpole's foreign policy. Walpole sits at a table dispensing gold, bank subscriptions, contracts, etc. On his right his brother Horace, in harlequin's waistcoat, welcomes a pantaloon who bows in the Spanish manner. This figure represents either the notorious Convention with Spain made in early January, or Benjamin Keene, the British plenipotentiary who had negotiated it. A Danish dog, suggesting the unpopular subsidy treaty with the court of Denmark, urinates on Horace's foot. In the background a crowd of sycophants file past.

The School of POLITICKS or Pantaloon made à MINISTER

convention with Spain.

Danish Subsidy.

Concedo tibi Virtutem, Tratandi, Guarantandi, Mediandi, Blunderandi, Confoundendi,
Corrumpendi, Pillagendi, stockjobbandi, Ruinandi, Dominandi, impune per totam Nationem.
Judæa Im. 3. 2d. ——
A. K. Nov. 1730.

61. BMC 2431   9 April 1739   Charles Mosley

The race is declared over. Fleury collects his trophies. Russia and Turkey are still fighting, with Austria about to join in against the Ottoman elephant. Among a wealth of detailed allusions, the British lion, held by a monkey, is mounted by a French fox. Walpole's negotiating mortar fires off another useless ambassador. 'Sturdy beggars' process with a merchants' petition; Britannia is beset by a Frenchman and a Spaniard; Benjamin Keene, the British representative at Madrid, has the Convention crammed down his throat; the British bulldog reposes on a French carpet. In the left background an English fleet defeats the Armada beneath a bust of Queen Elizabeth, while on the right its Hanoverian successor lies inactive before Minorca.

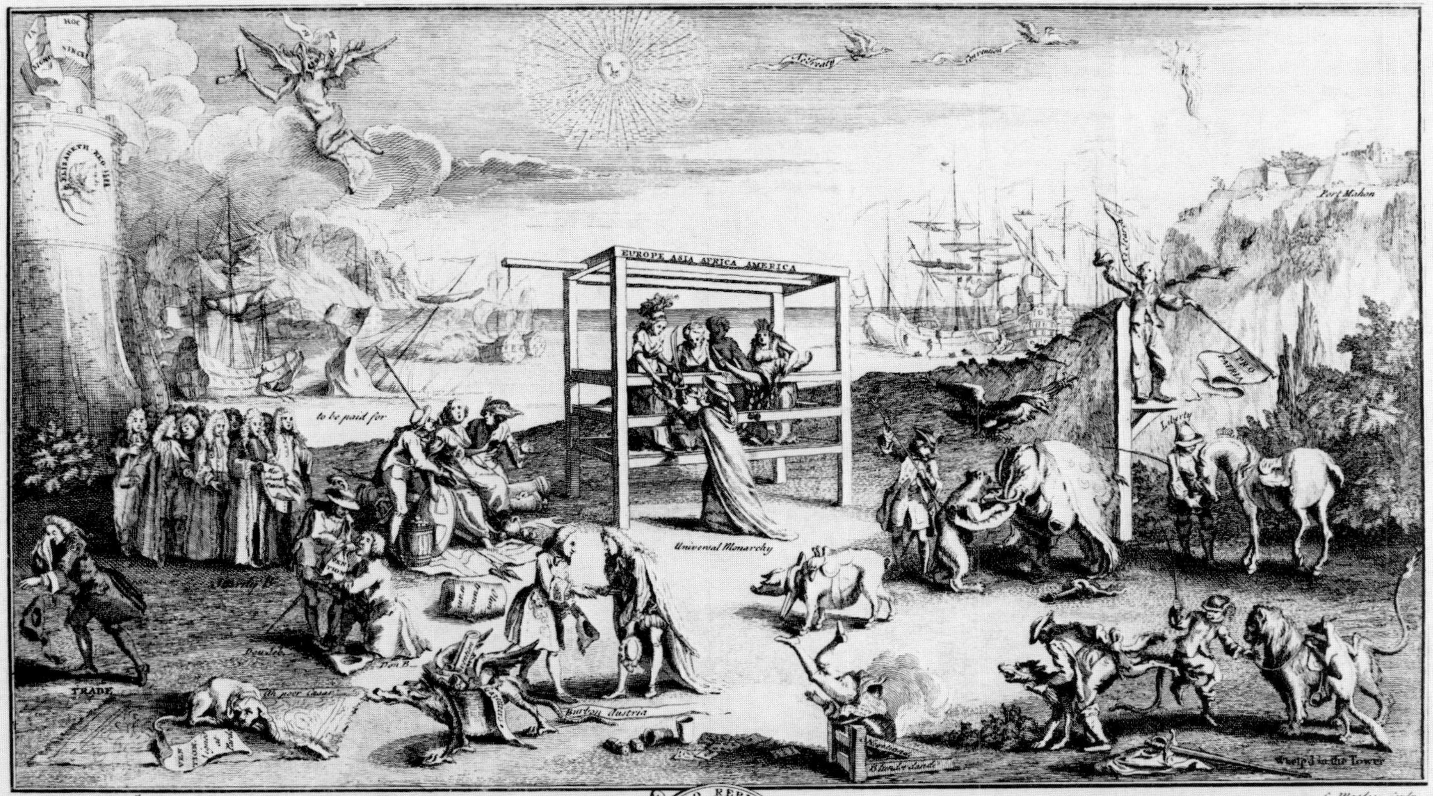
EUROPE ASIA AFRICA AMERICA
to be paid for
Universal Monarchy
Port Mahon
Liberty
TRADE

Publish'd April the 2d 1739 according to the late Act.

C. Mosley sculp

THE EUROPEAN RACE

Heat III.d ANNO DOM. MDCCXXXIX.

Inscrib'd to the Greatest Politician in Europe. By his most Obed.t Humble Serv.t An Englishman.

PRO REGE SEPE PRO REPUBLICA SEMPER

Behold, the former things are come to pass, and new things do I declare before they spring forth I tell you of them.

Isaiah the 42. Verse the 9.

See "Explanation" Lond. 1740. 12mo

62. BMC 2417   23 June 1739
    Walpole's appeasement contrasted with Oliver Cromwell's aggression. The
    original Dutch medal of 1655 had depicted Cromwell's success in compelling
    France and Spain to submit to England's power. This reproduction of the medal
    shows Cardinal Fleury inflicting a similar indignity on Walpole.

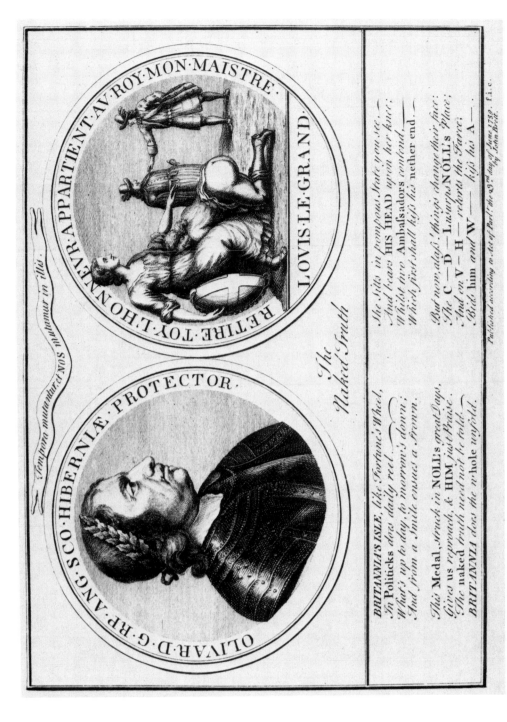

AV·ROY·MON·MAISTRE·APPARTIENT·L'HONNEVR·TOY·RETIRE·

LOVIS·LE·GRAND·

Tempora mutantur et nos mutamur in illis.

OLIVAR·D·G·RP·ANG·SCO·HIBERNIÆ·PROTECTOR·

The Naked Truth

BRITANNIA'S ISLE, like Fortune's Wheel,
In Politicks does daily reel.
What's up to day, to morrow's down;
And from a Smile evinces a Frown.

This Medal, struck in NOLL's great Days,
Gives us reproach, & HIM just Praise.
The naked truth need not be told:
BRITANNIA does the whole unfold.

She Jilts in pompous State you see,
And tears HIS HEAD upon her knee;
Whilst two Ambassadors contend,
Which first shall kiss his nether end.

But now, alas! things change their face:
The C—D—L usurps NOLL's Place;
And ev'n V—H—reborts the Farce;
Bids him and W—kiss his A—

Publish'd according to Act of Parl: the 29th day of June 1739. f.i.c. by John Brett.

63. BMC 2332   [1739]

Further comment on Walpole's pusillanimity. The British lion sleeps, the fleet lies inactive at Spithead, a seaman awaits his orders.

Spithead

I wait for Orders

The British Hercules

1737

64. BMC 2419   8 October 1739

The War of Jenkins' Ear begins unpromisingly. In the first scene the Dutch, who remained neutral and enjoyed a prosperous trade as a result, rifle the pockets of Britain while she fights with Spain. In the second Admiral Haddock fails to prevent the Spanish silver fleet arriving safely from America; in the foreground the British bull is baited by France and Spain while the Dutch attack it from the rear. In the third, Fleury and the Pretender plot an invasion of Britain, and in the fourth Haddock makes a feeble showing off Cadiz. Finally the threat of a siege of Gibraltar, comparable to that of 1728, is shown.

HOCUS POCUS: or the POLITICAL JUGLERS.

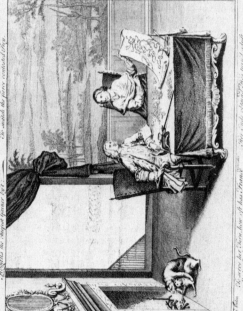

65. BMC 2434 1739 Charles Mosley

A rare attempt to defend or at least explain Walpole's foreign policy. In the first design the Spanish giant, having failed to deceive Britain with the 'Convention', sinks, belaboured by Walpole. In the second Walpole tries to escape from the clutches of Fleury, who intimidates him by pointing to the Jacobite threat. Next Walpole makes silent preparations by night to foil the French and Spanish giants. Finally Walpole confronts the combined powers while the Prince of Wales watches from behind a tree.

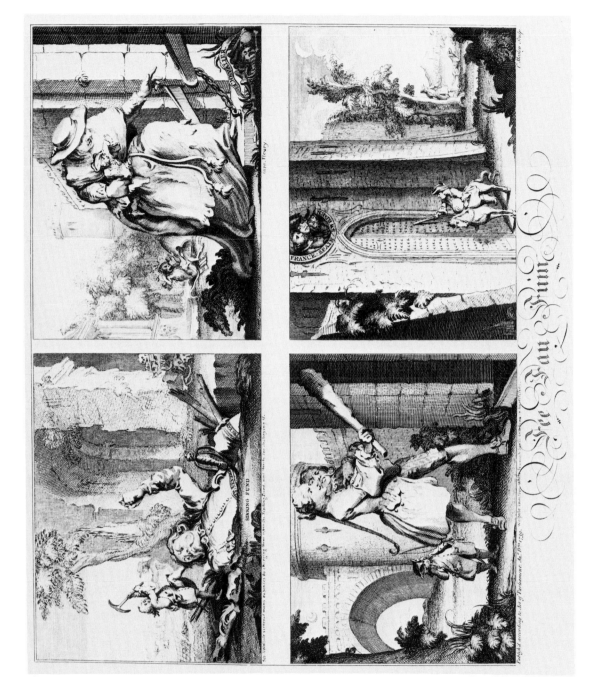

SINKING FUND

FRANCE SPAIN

Grav: Fleury

C. Mosley Sculp

The Wallpole Scheme of means of Service for Raising Mony from the Sinking Fund now Set to the Enquiring of...

Publish'd according to Act of Parliament Jan. 17th 1736

66. BMC 2458   [March] 1740   George Bickham
Walpole ironically compared with Caesar. Beneath and behind him is displayed the evidence of his blunders as a war minister.

Sig. R. Walpole.

The Statue of a
Great Man or the English Colossus.

G. B.-k-k sculp. N. ij. Oct. 1740.

Why Man, he doth bestride ij narrow World
like a Colossus, and we petty Men
Walk under his huge Legs, & peep about
So find ourselves dishonourable Graves.

Men at some times are Masters of their fates:
The fault, dear P— y is not in our Stars,
But in ourselves, that we are Underlings.

Shakespear.

Description.

The Colossus at Rhodes, a Statue of ij 4n 70 Cubits high, placed at ij Mouth of ij Harbour: one Man could not grasp its
Thumb with both his Arms. Its thighs were stretch'd out to such a Distance, that a large Ship Sailing might easily pass
into ij Port betwixt them. It was twelve Years a making, & cost 300 Talents (a Rhodian Talent is worth 322 Pounds 18
Shillings & 4 Pence in English Money). It stood 50 Years, & at last was thrown down in an Earth-quake. And from this
Coloss ij People of Rhodes were named Colossenses, & every Stature since of an unusual Magnitude is called Colossus.

67. BMC 2447   [1740]

Walpole from the rear. The caption, drawn from a spoof 'Chronicle of the Kings' makes the familiar comparison with Wolsey.

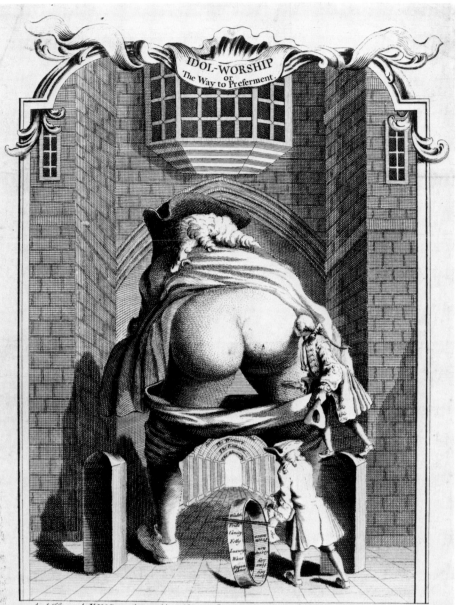

IDOL-WORSHIP
or
The Way to Preferment.

And Henry the KING made unto himself a great IDOL, the likeness of which was not in Heaven above, nor
in the Earth beneath; and he reared up his Head unto y̓ Clouds, & extended his Arm over all y̓ Land; His Legs also
were as y̓ Posts of a Gate, or as an Arch stretched forth over y̓ Doors of all y̓ Publick Offices in y̓ Land, & whosoever went out,
or whosoever came in, passed beneath, & with Idolatrous Reverence lift up their Eyes, & kissed y̓ Cheeks of y̓ Postern.

Chronicle of the Kings, page 31

68. BMC 2450   16 May 1740

A major development in domestic politics: the Duke of Argyll, the most powerful magnate in Scotland, defects to opposition. Here he takes his leave of the king and his mistress Lady Wallmoden.

So shines his Light before Mankind.
His Actions prove his honest Mind.
If in his Country's Cause he rise,
Debating Senates to advise.——

The Scotch Patriot
in Contrast, &c.

Unbrib'd, unaw'd, he dares impart
The honest Dictates of his Heart;
No ministerial Frown he fears,
But in his Virtue perseveres.—— 6th May, 1740

Publish'd by Thomas Fallerton May 16. 1740 Pr. 6.d

D. of Argyle resign'd his appointments May. 1740.

Integrity

69. BMC 2459 1740 Designed Francis Hayman, engraved Gerard Vandergucht
A panegyric of Walpole. He is shown being conducted to the Temple of Fame
by Burleigh; envy and other vices are repulsed by Minerva, while age and
beauty look on in admiration. The text offers a detailed defence of Walpole's
policies together with a poetic description of the scene and a comparison with
Elizabeth's appreciation of Burleigh.

F. Hayman Inv.   Burleigh   Walpole   G. Vander Gucht Sculp. 1740.

The PATRIOT-STATESMAN.

R. C.

1740.

70. BMC 2462 1740 George Bickham Jr.
A simple but brutal comparison of Walpole with Piers Gaveston, the favourite
of Edward II. The publication of the account of Gaveston's career which
accompanied it was patently meant as a comment on Walpole himself, who
here confesses his corruption and prepares for execution. Behind him is a
soldier of the standing army, carrying gold.

Tho' evil Ministers awhile, ——
May bask themselves in Fortune's smile;
They for their Crimes must soon or late
Like *Gaveston* submit to Fate.

71. BMC 2448   [June 1740]   Probably the work of Hubert Francois Gravelot
An effective satire on the *Craftsman*, which had been attacked by the
government press for its advocacy of place bills and other measures 'tinkering'
with the constitution. The *Craftsman* was foolish enough to object to this
expression and met with renewed mockery in consequence. The print was
published with a collection of the newspaper pieces in question.

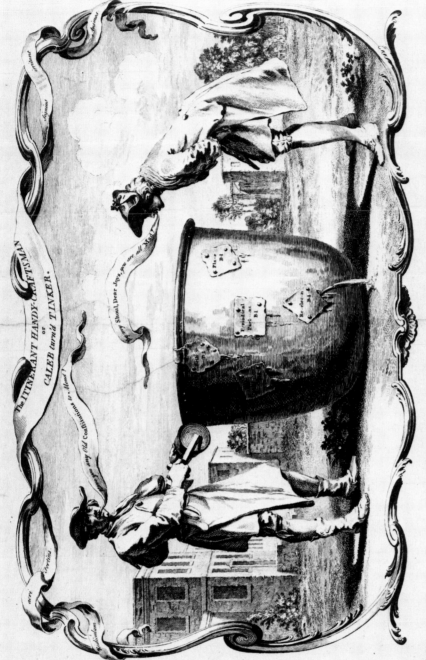

Faults still they find with This, or This, — As of Government was intended :
And something always is amiss : — For nothing else but to be Mended. —
Hudibras.

Publish'd according to Act of Parliament.

A minute's after Caleb Danvers Editor of the Craftsman.

72. BMC 2421   [1740]
   Admiral Vernon becomes a national hero with his victory at Portobello in November 1739. The Queen of Spain appeals to France for assistance. In the left corner, Spanish folly is displayed, in the right, British justice.

Britons love Peace, nor easily are rous'd;
yet when insults, and wrongs, and foul reproach,

Have mov'd their Souls to seek for retribution;
Perfidious Friends, and Enemies beware!

Than we chastize our Insolent Oppressors

France is my aid, the Universe my right

Queen of Spain

Whilst Spain by Folly, Castles builds, and places them in Th' Air,
Britain with Justice, arms, nevveroys retrys'd, and makes Commerce her Care.
Britain in vengeance fleet unites in West Indies 1740. Vernon took Port-Bello Nov. 1739

Adm. Vernon

Sec. Smollett. Ch. vi. b. 34. B. ii.

1740

73. BMC 2454   July 1740   George Bickham
The diplomatic and political significance of Vernon's victory displayed. Fleury points in despair at a portrait of the admiral. Walpole's head appears on a pole. The British flag flies triumphant.

The Preferment of the Barber's Block.

THE
Cardinal in the Dumps,
With the Head of the Colofus.
————— Age thou art Shamd!
Rome thou hast lost the Breed of Noble Bloods!
When went there by an Age since the great Flood,
But it was fam'd with more than one Man?
When could they fay, till now, who talk'd of Rome,
That her wide Walls encompafs'd but one Man?.

vernon   walpole   Fleury
According to Act July 1740. Sold at ye Black-moor's Head opposite Surry Street Strand.   July 1740

74. BMC 2422   July 1740   Charles Mosley
A shrewd opposition depiction of Vernon's victory, accompanying Richard
Glover's highly successful ballad. In his ship *Burford*, before Portobello,
Vernon and his men see the ghosts of Admiral Hosier and his crews, who had
perished in the ill-fated expedition to the West Indies during the 'phoney war'
of 1726. The failure of the expedition had been attributed to political
incompetence and treachery at home. The lesson on this occasion was clear.
Vernon had succeeded despite Walpole's war leadership, not because of it.

C. Mosley Sculp.

Admiral Hosier's Ghost.

To the Tune of Come and listen to my Ditty

I

As, near Porto Bello lying
On the gently swelling Flood,
At Midnight with Streamers flying
Our triumphant Navy rode;
There while Vernon sat all glorious
From the Spaniards' late Defeat,
And his Crews with Shouts victorious
Drank Success to England's Fleet.

II

On a sudden shrilly Sounding,
Hideous Yells & Shrieks were heard;
Then, each Heart with Fear confounding,
A sad Troop of Ghosts appear'd.
All in dreary Hammocks shrouded,
Which for Winding sheets they wore,
And with Looks by Sorrow clouded,
Frowning on that hostile Shore.

III

On them gleam'd the Moon's wan lustre
When the Shade of Hosier brave,
His pale Bands was seen to muster
Rising from their watry Grave.
O'er the glimmering Wave he hied him,
Where the Burford reard her Sail,
With three thousand Ghosts beside him,
And in Groans did Vernon hail.

IV

Heed, oh heed our fatal Story!
I am Hosier's injur'd Ghost.
You, who now have purchas'd Glory
At this Place where I was lost;
Though in Porto Bello's ruin
You now triumph free from Fears,
When, you think on our undoing,
You will mix your Joy with Tears.

V

See these mournful Spectres sweeping
Ghastly o'er this hated Wave,
Whose wan Cheeks are stain'd with weeping
These were English Captains brave.
Mark those Numbers pale and horrid,
Who were once my Sailors bold,
Lo, each hangs his drooping forehead,
While his dismal Fate is told.

VI

[...] twenty Sail attended
[...] this Spanish Town affright;
[...] ng then its Wealth defended
[...] my Orders not to fight;
[...] hat in this rolling Ocean,
[...] d cast them with Disdain,
[...] beyd my Heart's warm Motion
[...] quell'd the Pride of Spain.

VII

But with twenty Ships had done,
What thou brave and happy Vernon,
Hast atchiev'd with Six alone,
Then the Bastimento's never
To have fall'n my Country crying
He has play'd an English Part,
Had been better far than dying
Of this gallant Train had been

VIII

Thus like thee, proud Spain dismaying
And her Galleons leading home,
Though condemn'd for Disobeying
I had met a milder Doom,
To have fall'n my Country crying
He has play'd an English Part,
Had been better far than dying
Of a griev'd and broken Heart.

IX

Unrepining at thy Glory,
Thy successful arms we hail;
But remember our sad Story,
And let Hosier's wrongs prevail.
Sent in this foul clime to languish,
Think what thousands fell in vain,
Wasted with disease and anguish,
Not in glorious battle slain.

X

Hence with all my train attending
From their oozy tombs below,
Through the hoary foam ascending,
Here I feed my constant woe,
Here the Bastimento's viewing,
We recal our shameful doom,
And our plaintive cries renewing,
Wander through the midnight gloom.

XI

For those wan spirits forever mourning,
Shall we roam depriv'd of rest,
If to Britain's shores returning,
You neglect my just request;
After this proud foe subduing,
When your patriot friends you see,
Think on vengeance for my ruin,
And for England sham'd in me.

Publish'd according to Act of Parliament July' 1740

July 1740

75. BMC 2437 [1740]

Walpole's pusillanimity once again displayed. The British lion has its eyes pecked out by a French cock while a Frenchman looks on. A British sailor urges the lion on, a bulldog waits to be unleashed, a cannon is in readiness: only a vigorous war leader is needed to set all in motion.

The Gallic Cock and English Lyon or A Touch of the Times. ― Vernon once took to take Porto bello with six ships 1739.

Dedicated to the Brave Admiral Vernon and all true Britons ~ by Jack Tarpaulin ~ 1739

1739/40

The Gallic Cock no way can find
To bait the Lyon, but is Kind:
He otherwise from the Lyon begs,
But leaves to tear him all to rags.

Should English courage break the Chain,
Gallia would play her tricks in vain;
By Havock, wounds, and slaughter rent,
Her broken Faith she'd soon repent.

Then let Britannia's Fleets advance
And curb the Insolence of France;
For Vengeance arm, and bravely dare
In Thunder to proclaim the War.

76.	BMC 2420	13 September 1740	Charles Mosley
The consequences of Argyll's defection are examined in three stages. In the foreground Walpole dispatches the devil and a pack-horse loaded with bribes to recover Scotland. The devil arrives before Edinburgh and attempts to distribute his gold while the Duke looks on. Finally Argyll makes an inspiring speech to a group of virtuous Scots who rejoice at his independence. The Campbell electoral machine in Scotland was an important part of the Walpole system; though Argyll was replaced by his brother Islay, the general election of 1741 was to bring about a substantial and strategically crucial reduction in Walpole's parliamentary majority.

THE STATE PACK-HORSE

In this Mysterious, Mythologic Scene,
Pitier poach players Speaks than Bronze or Rime;
Let Light and Shade before your Eyes Defcend,
His Country, Ki..., and the Devil's Friend.

Vi: Metamorphosis you've oft been told,
Here, a Work British. One you may behold;
His Vices had his Errand done foretold,
Are told his faith and Liberty's Well.

77. BMC 2440   25 November 1740   Charles Mosley
     An elaborate mixture of history and prophecy. The calendar begins with an
     innocuous picture of the Thames frost fair held in the exceptionally severe
     winter of 1739–40, and ends by predicting for November a political onslaught
     on Walpole at Westminster, and for December a demonstration by Fleury of
     his almost mystical powers of diplomacy before the entranced monarchs of
     Europe. The central panel shows the three sovereigns, Frederick William I,
     Charles VI and Anne, all of whom died in the course of this year, passing into
     the care of Charon.

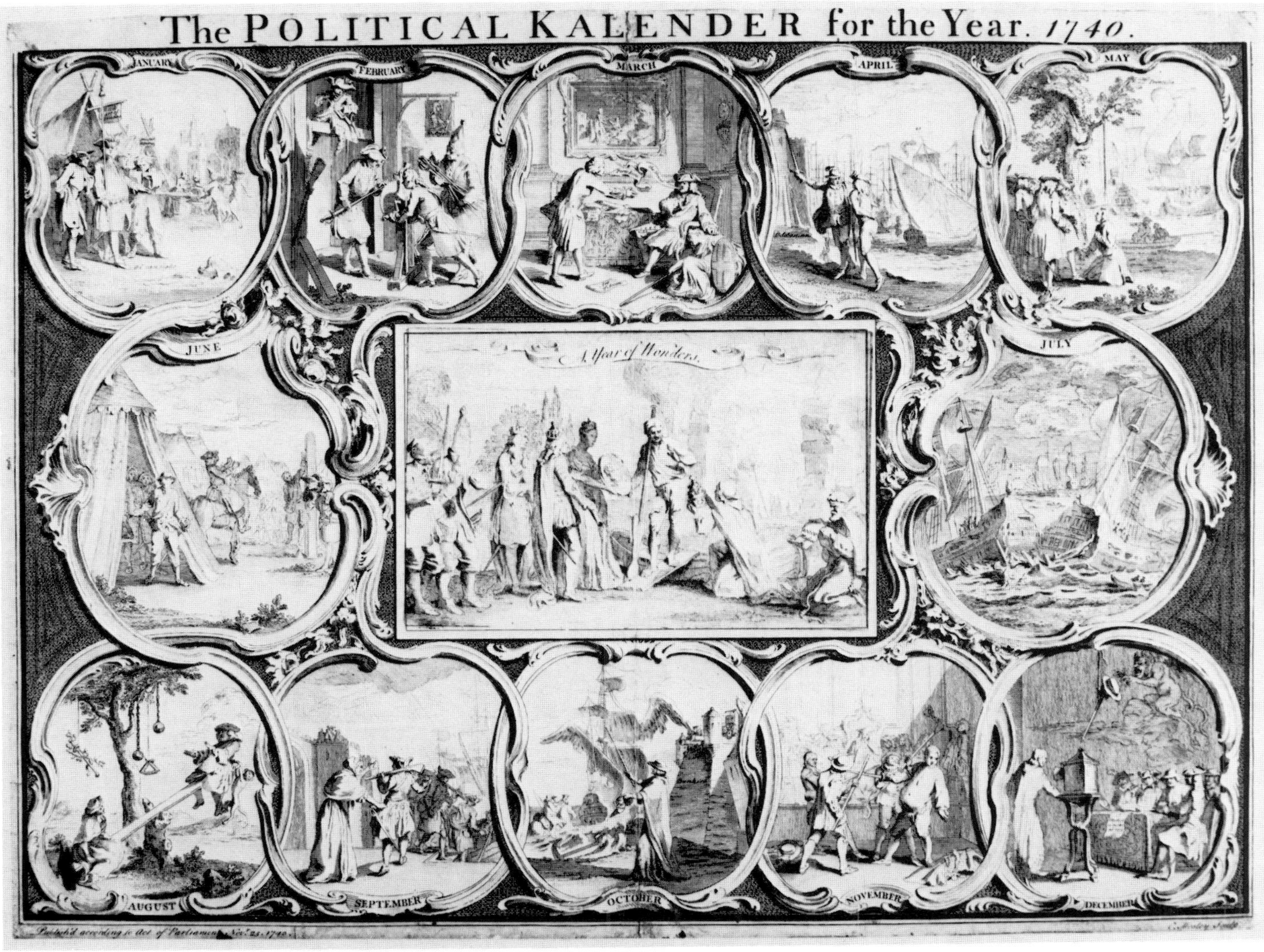
The POLITICAL KALENDER for the Year. 1740.
JANUARY
FEBRUARY
MARCH
APRIL
MAY
JUNE
A Year of Wonders.
JULY
AUGUST
SEPTEMBER
OCTOBER
NOVEMBER
DECEMBER
Publish'd according to Act of Parliament Novr. 25. 1740.

78. BMC 2418   6 December 1740

Walpole is blamed for the generally unpromising start to the war with Spain. (Top left) the war is proclaimed, (top centre) the English fleet lies inactive while the Spanish treasure fleet is safely brought home, (top right) Admiral Vernon achieves his great victory at Portobello. (Bottom left) the royal navy fails to prevent the French and Spanish fleets departing for the West Indies, (bottom centre) enemy raiders decimate British merchant shipping, (bottom right) Admiral Haddock is ordered to abandon his blockade of Cadiz. In the centre panel England's evil genius corrupts Walpole and his ministry.

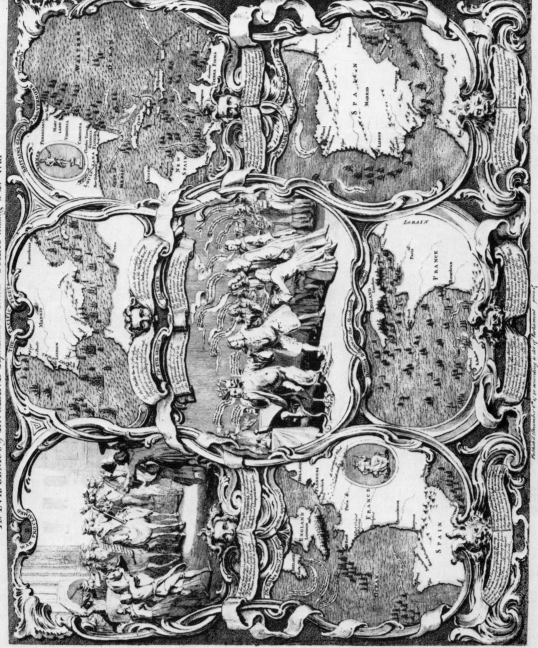

The EVIL GENIUS of ENGLAND Represented in Several Scenes relating to the War

79.   BMC 2473   [c.1740]   Thomas Gardner
      A sinister threat to Walpole. He is offered a bribe while an avenging figure
      stands by with a rope.

Tho. Gardner Sculp

_____ *Design what e'er we will,*
There is a Fate which over-rules us still.

Spect.

80. BMC 2439   9 January 1741   Hubert Francois Gravelot?

An election print with the general election of 1741 in prospect. Walpole is carried through the mire while to the right those who have already been corrupted by it attempt to make themselves more presentable. In the background canvassing takes place. One candidate who is taking money from Britannia's pocket has an attentive audience; another offering the cap of liberty is rejected.

Sr. Rob. Walpole

THE DEVIL UPON TWO STICKS

To the worthy Electors of Great Britain this Print

is humbly inscribed and the following Verses are addressd by their Friend & Countryman

Is it not, oh my Friends, a most culpable thing,
So exalt any Villain except in a String?
What then must they brand him perfectly evil,
With constant supporters who furnish the Devil!
Through Dirt, without Danger, these bear him along
Nor to him the right way is more safe than the wrong —
But Shear apert Critic, in love with Dispute,
Exclaim that the Picture & Title don't suit,
Where's the Horns, the cleft foot, & the sad sable hue
That depicture the Devil ad vivum to Vein?
And then, his Supporters seem rational Creatures!
Have two sticks, you dul Sot, such a shape & such Features?
Be Patient dear Sir, and in brief I reply
That tis Belial Ide show by that thing rais'd so high,
And will Horns and cleft feet just Ideas excite
Of the Qualities whitame ascrib'd to that Spright?
He hollow & false wore a Specious outside,
And his tongue the designs of his Bosom bely'd;
The worst he could make to appear the best Reason
To dash faithfull Councel and make it seem Treason
His thoughts low and mean, still industrious to vice,
Like a Dastant he trembled at honest advice;
So basely averse to each Deed truly great,
Kid advise a lame peace tho' it shackle the State
Or a War so much like it that no one can see
The least mark of distinction between them but he:

Of these bright perfections, that air & that Dress
Are Symbols most proper the World must confess.
These, these in such Colours depicture the Mind
That none can mistake it but those who are blind.
And whoe'er with the share of Attention that's due
These mystic Supporters that bear him shall veiw,
Must think thus with himself — Watercoopis. space —
These two things then for certain Imprimis have Place
Minus I see. These are Tools only mov'd by the Devil,
To work his dark purpose and bring about Evil:
Men therefore they are not, yet surely 'twas meant
Thus shap'd and thus dress'd they should Men represent,
That sometimes they should speak but meer Engines we know
Can produce nothing more than a yes or a no —
Now I say the Idea these musings must fix,
Will be that of a Faggot and ergo two Sticks.
But I've done with the Critic — and now oh my Friends!
Fullfill my warm wish that your welfare intends.
The great Now is the time these Supports to withdraw
And three Kingdoms no longer proud Belial shall Awe —
Down, down then at once the great Idol must fall,
And thenceforth be no more than a Dagon or Baal;
For hell surely expire in that great complication
Of Dirt, which is now call'd the state of the Nation.

* Miltons Paradise lost Book 2d.

* Members who Voted for the Excise & against the Convention
 A.y. 1733.   1739
ll Vigourous Measures
cc Candidates

9 Jan. 1740/1

Publish'd according to Act of Parliament January the 9. 1741.

81. BMC 2463   March 1741   George Bickham

The approach of continental war, with the death of the Emperor Charles VI and the accession of Maria Theresa to the Austrian throne. On the left George II plays see-saw with her enemy the future Bavarian Emperor for whose election he was to vote in his capacity as elector of Hanover. Walpole, one foot in the political grave, does his best to shackle his own navy and ignores a petitioning merchant. In the centre Frederick of Prussia occupies Silesia, spurning Maria Theresa and her husband, the Grand Duke of Tuscany, to the left. On the right the powers of Europe negotiate in this crisis. Fleury and the King of France discuss the Pragmatic Sanction, guaranteeing Maria Theresa's inheritance of her father's lands. The King and Queen of Spain urge war, while Holland remains neutral. The abdicated King of Corsica lies on the ground.

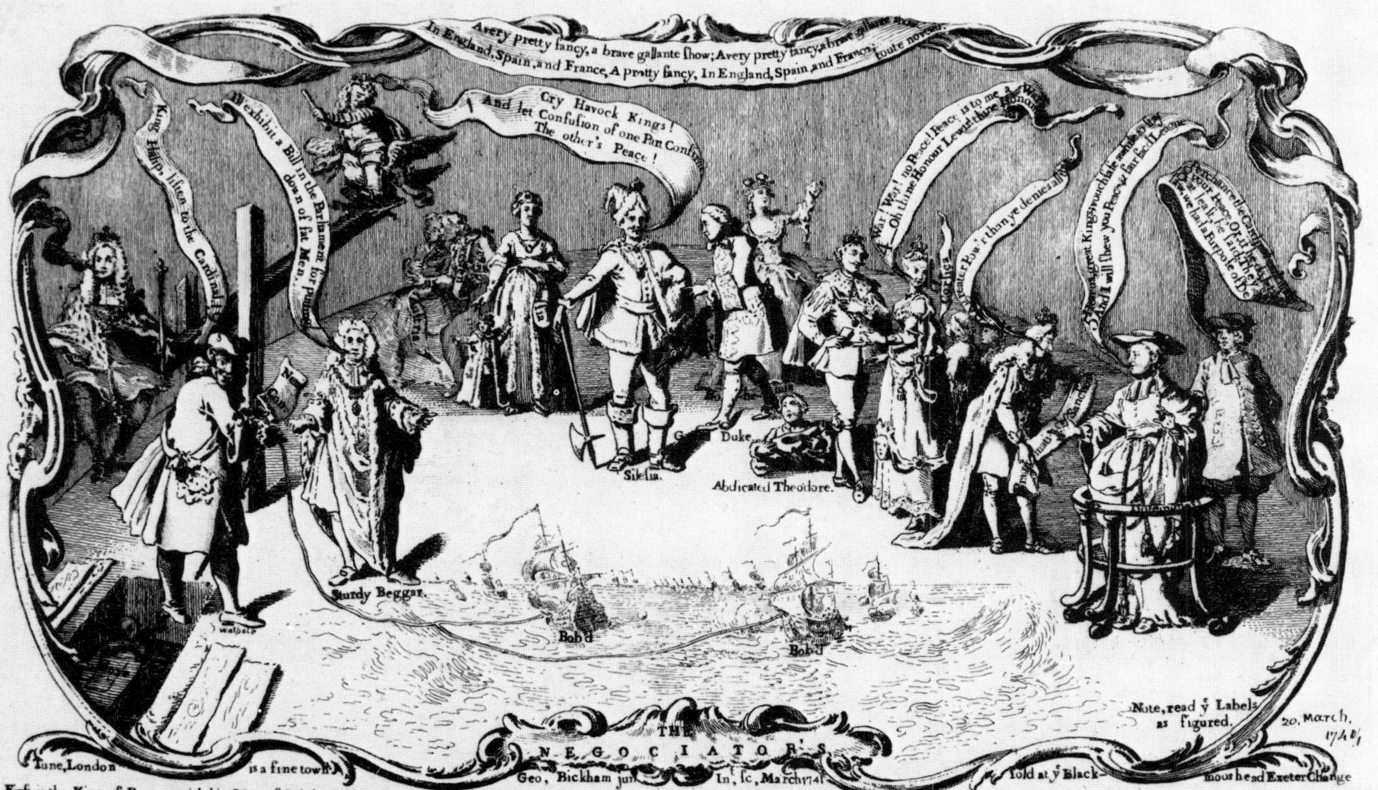
A very pretty fancy, a brave gallante show; A very pretty fancy, a brave gallante show
In England, Spain, and France, A pretty fancy, In England, Spain and France
Cry Havock Kings!
And let Confusion of one Part Confirm
The other's Peace!
Sturdy Beggar.
Silesia.
Duke
Abdicated Theodore.
Bob'd
Bob'd
Note, read ye Labels
as figured.
20. March.
1740/1
THE
NEGOCIATOR'S
Tune, London is a fine town
Geo, Bickham jun In t, sc, March 1741 sold at ye Black-moors head Exeter Change

1 First is the King of Pru—a with his Men of Might,
Swears he's got Silesia, whether wrong or wright:
2 Then the King of B—t—n, with an Army brave,
Vows he will the Empire to Tuscany Save.

3 Than the King of F—ncee, with Pragmatick Show,
Says he'll make 'em dancee, with a toute noveau;
4 But the Queen of Sp—nee, turbulunt and proud,
Is resolv'd to gainue, Italy aloud.

5 Cardinal de Fl—ry, and the British Bob, 6
Now are both securee, from a Roguish Job:
7 Aldurmen in Petto, seek their private Ends,
Whilst the Dutchman 8 never, is a friend to friends.

Then the Duke of Tuscany, and his worthy Queen
And great Russia's Regen, with little John is seen;
The Po—sh King, and C—los of Corsica that's sold,
Poor Theodore, and Austria with Sweden the bold.

Walpole called the Petitioners against the Excise Bill. 'Sturdy Beggars'. Coxe's Walpole, ch. 41. p401.

See this Plate altered Feb. 1742.

82. BMC 2479   [February] 1741

The court's opening salvo in a protracted battle of the prints, caused by the opposition's discomfiture in February 1741 when a motion to address the crown for Walpole's removal was heavily defeated in the Commons. The opposition coach is shown running out of control. Argyll is astride the lead-horse, with his despised friend Bubb Dodington underfoot; on the box is Chesterfield, at the rear Cobham, and behind him on horseback George Lyttelton. Carteret desperately attempts to leave the coach. Samuel Sandys, who actually put the motion, waves his arms in despair. In the centre the 'patriot bishop' Smalbrook of Lichfield bows obsequiously, and on the left Pulteney and a procession of opposition Whigs watch with dismay.

The MOTION.

TREASURY

WHITEHALL

I.
WHO be dat de Box do fit on?
  'Tis *John*, the Hero of *North-Britain*,
Who our of Place, does Place-men spit on,
                              Doodle, &c.

II.
Between his Legs de Spaniel Curr fee,
Tho' now he growle at *Bob* so fierce,
Yet he fawn'd on him once in *Doggerel* Verse,
                              Doodle, &c.

III.
And who be dat *Postilion* there,
Who drive o'er all and no Man spare?
'Tis *Ph——p E——le* — of here and there,
                              Doodle, &c.

IV.
But pray who in de Coaché sit-a?
  'Tis honest *J——my C——r——ritta*,
Who want in place again to git-a,
                              Doodle, &c.

V.
Who's dat behind? 'tis *Dicky Cobby*,
Who first wou'd have hang'd, and then try'd *Bobby*,
Ah, was not that a pretty Jobb-e?
                              Doodle, &c.

VI.
Who's dat who ride aftride de Poney,
So long, so lank, so lean, and bony?
O he be de great Orator *Little-Stony*,
                              Doodle, &c.

VII.
Close by stands *Billy* of all *Bob*'s Foes,
De wittest sur in Verse, and Prose;
How he lead de Puppies by de Nose?
                              Doodle, &c.

VIII.
Who's he dat lift up both his Handes?
O that's his Wisdom Squire *S——*,
O de Place-Bill drop! O de Army standes!
                              Doodle, &c.

IX.
What Parson's he dat bow so civil?
O dat's de Bishop who split the Devil,
And made a Devil and a half, and half a Devil,
                              Doodle, &c.

X.
So, Sirs, me have shewn you all de *Hero*'s,
Who put you together by the Ear-os,
And frighten you so with groundless Fear-os,
                              Doodle, &c.

Printed for T. COOPER, at the *Globe* in *Pater-
noster-Row*, 1741.

Published according to Act of Parliament.

Price Three-Pence.

83. BMC 2491   2 March 1741

The opposition's initial reply to *The Motion* offered the supposed reason for its defeat (not as the MS. addition to the print suggests, for its attempt). Walpole drives a coach in which the Duke of Cumberland dispenses army commissions. Lord Hervey with a fan on a wooden horse, brings up the rear. In the foreground Conyers Middleton displays his newly published life of Cicero, dedicated to Hervey. Centre and left, Walpole's supporters in the church, the law and the army urge him on, for fear of losing their wages, while on the extreme right breathless M.P.s arrive to vote for the minister. A topical detail is the presence in the centre of Argyll, who had publicly stated his inability over many years to promote officers without political connections and who is here seen fruitlessly offering his nominations to Walpole.

The R E A S O N.

.of the Motion for Walpole's dismissal.

W. Cowper, Walfell fce.

I.
WHO be dat de Box do sit on?
Dat's de Driver of Great-Britain —— Walpole.
Whom all de Patriots do fpit on,
Doodle, &c.

II.
And der's young Billy in the Landau,
Wid new Co——ssions in his Paw,
Dat make de Mongrel M——s withdraw,
Doodle, &c.

III.
Who is dat on Fore-horse riding?
'Tis he de Coachman does confide in,
Of all de Hackneys to have de guiding,
Doodle, &c.

IV.
See how de Place-men push on Bubber,
To fave der Place, and do der Jobber
Begar dey care not who dey robbe,
Doodle, &c.

V.
Who be dat wid five and forty,
So grave, fo wife, and eke fo dirty?
O dat's der Hero of de Nortb, —— Argyle.
Doodle, &c.

VI.
See he bends with low Submiffion,
All thefe I'll make——but make Petition,
Dat you will give dem all C——m——n, Doodle, &c.

VII.
Dat painted Butterfly fo prim-a,
On wooden Pegafus fo trim-a, L.Hervey, Wingbread.
Is something——nothing——'tis a Whim-a,
Doodle, &c.

VIII.
Here be Doctor Middle——fexty,
Leading Ralpho de C——t Poney,
Wid de Trath dey get der Money,
Doodle, &c.

IX.
See de B——ps in der Lawn-a,
By de love of Mammon drawn-a,
On der Coachman how dey fawn-a]
Doodle, &c.

X.
Dere be Groom and Stable-Sweeper,
Chamber-Loon, and de Houfe-keeper,
Praying der Wages mayn't run deeper,
Doodle, &c.

XI.
And dere is John, de long Dragoon Sir,
Hark, he fwears and bluffers Zonce Sir,
If dey clamour, knock 'em down Sir,
Doodle, &c.

Printed for T. Cooper, at the Globe in Pater-nofter-Row, 1741. Feb. 13
Publifh'd according to Act of Parliament. (Price Six-pence.)

84. BMC 2484 7 March 1741

Another early riposte to *The Motion*. Walpole's money chest (pulled by a troop of excisemen) rolls remorselessly over liberty and trade in its tax-gathering progress. Walpole himself rides on top, disembowelling the sinking fund as he goes; his brother sits behind and the government's supporters in the church and the press bring up the rear. In the foreground the booty is dispensed to the Law (left), the Church (right), the army (extreme left) and revenue officers (extreme right). In the distance the Bourbon fleets depart for the West Indies while the British fleet lies inactive in Torbay.

THE GROUNDS.

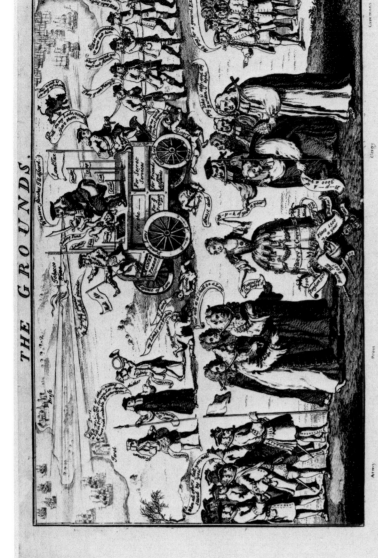

Sold at the Print and Pamphlet-Shops of *London* and *Westminster*. Publish'd according to Act of Parliament, *March* 7, 1741. (Price Fourpence.)

Army.

I.

VAT be dat Machine do make de Folk groan-é?
It be de Invention of de old Fox Volponé,
To crush de People's Spirit, and squeeze out deir Money,
                                            Doodle, doodle, do.

II.

Who be de big Man dat de Engine don't fit on?
He be de *great Projector of Great Britain*, Sir *R. Walpole*;
Whom all Men, except de *Placemen*, do spit on.
                                            Doodle, &c.

III.

He find out Contrivances, never before
Were practic'd to make dem both humble and poor;
'Tis for *all deir Gads* dat he do't, to be sure.
                                            Doodle, &c.

IV.

He let de Manufacture sink, and to ruin run Trade,
Yet Year after Year, heavy Taxes are laid;
And, vat be still more provoking, de huge Debts lie unpaid.
                                            Doodle, &c.

V.

He put all de best Post in his Family's Hands,
Lay out de Millions in Houses, and purchasing Lands,
And give no Account, wen de Nation demands.
                                            Doodle, &c.

Priess

VI.

To carry on his Designs, he make dem maintain,
More Officers Civil dan in both *France* and *Spain*,
And double de Army, in any past Reign.
                                            Doodle, &c.

VII.

Dem fill more securely, and surely to chouse,
He vid *Placemen* and *Pensioners* fill up de House;
So deir Liberty itself now lies at his Dispose.
                                            Doodle, &c.

VIII.

In Haste to swallow all, he did silly devise
Dat notable Project, call'd de *Excise*,
Wich fill de whole Nation, vid Rage and Surprise.
                                            Doodle, &c.

IX.

D: *List* to encrease, a whole ninth Part and more,
He model de G—n A—t, dat make tousands poor;
Yet kaveth de Evil, just de same as before.
                                            Doodle, &c.

X.

De Register Bill, he take lately in Hand,
Dat de Forces by Sea, as well as by Land,
Might be Slaves to his Will and despotic Command.
                                            Doodle, &c.

Clergy

XI.

Fifteen Years he with-hold dem from curbing deir Foes,
Who plunder and fearch dem; then, to add to deir Woes,
In Place of *Redress*, wou'd de *Convention* impose.
                                            Doodle, &c.

XII.

Brave *Vernon* resolve deir proud Enemies Ruin;
But, instead of sending any Forces to him,
Both de *French* and *Spanish* Fleets verre let loose to undo him.
                                            Doodle, &c.

XIII.

Who be de human Puppies, dat de Engine do draw?
Dey be his Tools, wid whom *all be say* pass for *Law*,
And but for whom he wou'd soon fall under Justice's Claw.
                                            Doodle, &c.

XIV.

Who be de Groupes of Swordmen, Gownsmen and other dat escort him?
Dey be his Creatures in de State, Church, Army and Revenue, dat court him;
For, as dey depend on him, dey must needs support him.
                                            Doodle, &c.

XV.

Thus you see all des Bands be at his Devotion;
And dat de Danger fear'd from him be no idle Notion:
Judge den, if dere was not de *Grounds* for de *Motion*,
                                            Doodle, doodle, d.

Commons

85. BMC 2486   [March] 1741
A sequel to *The Motion*, showing Walpole surviving the attacks of his enemies. The latter are as portrayed in the earlier print, except that Cobham does not appear. There is also one significant addition. In the foreground the Jacobite leader William Shippen declares his intention of not meddling; it was in fact mainly the refusal of the Tories to support the opposition's personal attack on Walpole which caused its defeat. In the background Walpole's enemies, like Sisyphus, can make no progress.

THE ACQUITAL.

I.
WHO be He dat ftand alone-a,
Midft de Darts, dat fhower down-a
Thick as Hail, yet hurt by none? *Doodle, &c.*

II.
O! dar be de gallant *Bobby*, *Walpole*
Whom de *Mal-contents* wou'd mob-e,
And of his Fame and *Places* rob-e. *Doodle, &c.*

III.
Vat dey fhoot at him vid deir Bows-a?
Dey be de fierceft of his Foes-a,
Who out of *Place* his Schemes oppofe-a. *Doodle, &c.*

IV.
Envious of his higher Merit,
Dey had a *Motion* of de Spirit,
Such as moft *Patriots* inherit. *Doodle, &c.*

V.
But how unluckily they fped-a,
All *Europe* has by dis Time read-a:
De *Party* now hang down dere Head-ah! *Doodle, &c.*

VI.
L---d *J---n*, a heavy Dart firft drew; *Coufaret*
He fhot; bit, fhooting much afkew,
On one Side de Arrow flew. *Doodle, &c.*

VII.
De fecond Archer in de File, *Argyle*
Prepar'd an Arrow full of *Gyle*:
But fhot it o'er his Head a Mile. *Doodle, &c.*

VIII.
De *Bump* dipp'd his Shaft in Gall, *Sandys*
And vow'd therewith to make him fall; *by Carteret*
But fall himfelf, de Jeft of all. *Doodle, &c.*

IX.
His *William* next a Dart let fly;
He aim'd to hit him in de Eye,
But, vid his Hand, *Bob* put it by, *Doodle, &c.*

X.
As *Daddy* thought to pierce him through, *Sandys*
Snap went de String; at which his Bow, *Pulteney*
For very Rage, he broke in two. *Doodle, &c.*

XI.
Lank *Gwegy* made his beft Effort, *Littleton*
And lean'd on *Naddy* for Support;
But, waning Strength, de Shaft fell fhort. *Doodle, &c.*

XII.
Den *Billy*, muftering all his Force, *Pulteney*
An Arrow fhot, deir laft Refource;
Which miffing, made de Squire to curfe. *Doodle, &c.*

XIII.
On dis *Bob's* Friends give all de Shout:
His Foes, no few, turn Tail about;
And for mere Rage and Shame run out. *Doodle, &c.*

XIV.
Dey drop deir Arrows and deir Bows;
Dey tumble over Friends and Foes;
Some break deir Shin, and fome deir Nofe. *Doodle, &c.*

XV.
Thus ended this long threaten'd Storm,
Rais'd to demolifh *Bob* in Form:
But thofe who watch, themfelves catch Harm. *Doodle, &c.*

Printed for T. Cooper, at the Globe, in Paternofter-Row, 1741. Publifh'd according to Act of Parliament. Price Six Pence.

86. BMC 2487   26 March 1741

The opposition's humiliation in February is further exploited. Faction is laid to rest as Sandys and Richard Glover officiate. Walpole and his friends jeer. The verses below add one new element in the propaganda war: in stanza xi, Perkin (Charles Edward) is cited in an attempt to associate the cause of Jacobitism with Walpole's enemies.

The FUNERAL of FACTION.

Funerals perform'd by Squire J—ds and the best Shammy Gloves by Leonidas.

I.

GOD prosper long our noble King,
  Our Lives and Safeties all ;
A woeful Motion lately did
  In *Westminster* befall.

II.

To drive Sir R—— from the State
  Bald C—p—l took his Way,
The Child may laugh that is unborn
  The Motion of that Day.

III.

This noble P—— with Anger shook,
  A Vow to God did make,
That he would rout Sir R—— out,
  And make all Place-men quake.

IV.

These Tidings to Sir R—— came,
  That on a certain Day
This doughty P—— and Squire S——ds
  Would his Indictment lay.

V.

The Knight undaunted sent them Word,
  He would assist their Sport,
An'l, trusting on his Innocence,
  Did to the House resort.

VI.

The angry Curs began to bark,
  And snarl upon the Chair ;
On *Thursday* they began their Cry,
  When Day-light did appear.

VII.

The noisy Yea's were on the Left,
  Not able to endure :
The Nay's were muster'd on the Right,
  In their just Cause secure.

VIII.

All Day they fought it hand to hand,
  The *Tories* left the Plain,
And, e're the Noon of Night was past,
  Th'unruly Beast was slain.

IX.

Thus Faction yielded up the Ghost
  In Rage, Despair, and Pain ;
A rich old Widow then perceiv'd
  Her darling Son was slain.

X.

Who strait invites his nearest Kin,
  This dismal Death to rue,
And she herself chief Mourner is,
  All this we know is true.

XI.

This heavy News to *Perkin* came,
  Alas ! alas ! said he ;
I've now no Hopes in old *England*,
  The Pope must comfort me.

XII.

God save the King, and bless the Land
  In Plenty, Joy and Peace ;
And grant, henceforth that foul Debate
  In either House may cease.   (Price Six-pence.)

Printed for T. Cooper, at the Globe in *Pater-noster-Row*, 1741.

Publish'd according to Act of Parliament.

87. BMC 2488   7 April 1741

A further contribution to *The Motion* series, revealing the result of the political conflict in the Lords. Walpole is protected from justice by his parliamentary majority, the placemen, the army and the revenue officers, while Britannia urges the opposition to continue its campaign. Though the motion put in the Lords met with the same fate as that in the Commons, opposition peers exercised their right to register a formal protest, which was subsequently published in the press.

THE PROTEST

W—to H—ll

Fr—a—y

I.

WHO be de Noble Lady dere,
  Dat seem as if she go to tear
Vulpes, from his Elbow-Chair?
        Doodle, &c.

II.

O! Dat be *Justice*, Lovely Dame!
  Sent, in fair *Britannia's* Name,
To 'venge her injur'd *Rights*, and *Fame*.
        Doodle, &c.

III.

And who be She dat near her stand?
  Dat be *Maj. Vol's* Truly Friend,
Who save him out of *Justice* Hand.
        Doodle, &c.

IV.

Her Father, *Placeman*, by her Side,
  Bloated up vid Wealth and Pride,
Seemeth *Justice* to deride.
        Doodle, &c.

V.

Vat Smock-face Soldier dat voud charm-e?
  'Tis *Maj's* Son, call'd *Standing-Army*,
To keep, both *Vol* and Her, from Harm-e.
        Doodle, &c.

VI.

And who de oder Prop, behind?
  He's too of Standing-Army kind,
Excise, a huge, voracious Hind.
        Doodle, &c.

VII.

Who be She shoot vid de Bow?
  Dat be *Minority*, who go
Vol, and his Schemes, to overthrow.
        Doodle, &c.

VIII.

She long Time since had made him smart,
  But thriveless *Maj* still take his Part,
And, vid her Shield, put by de Dart.
        Doodle, &c.

IX.

Provok'd at last, *Min* cry'd, " thou Elf
  " Remove thy Shield, *Vol* hires for Pelf,
  " And let the Fox defend himself."
        Doodle, &c.

X.

" I'll ne'er resign him, *Maj* reply'd,
  " To be, by You or *Justice*, try'd:
  " He's much securer by my Side.
        Doodle, &c.

XI.

" If you expect I'll act so ill
  " By *Vally*, while he pays me well,
  " You roll de Stone 'gainst de Hill."
        Doodle, &c.

XII.

Min, finding 'twas in vain to sue,
  Or hope Redress from such a Crew,
Made her *Protest*, and so withdrew.
        Doodle, &c.

Published according to Act of Parliament, *April* the 7th 1741, and Sold by *J. Tinney*, at the Golden Lion, in *Fleet-Street*, and at the Print and Pamphlet-Shops.

Price 6d. 1741.

88. BMC 2489   21 April 1741
In the wake of *The Motion* Walpole's supporters go on the offensive. A noisy but baffled opposition looks on as Walpole defies the rage of party and plans a renewed war campaign – a rare attempt to show him as a resolute and vigorous war minister.

TRUTH and MODERATION.

'MIDST home-bred Feuds and foreign sur-
    turn'd Jars,
The Discontents of Party, sordid Strife,
Foul rais'd Dissensions, ill-tim'd Contumely,
Behold the Man! serene as Mid-day Sun,
Gentle as genial Showers, calm as *Zephyrs*,

When govern'd by the sweetest Influences
  Of Heav'n-born *Pleasure*,
How vain's their Thought, whole avaricious Eyes
Survey with Longings those abundant Gains
The Pride of *Britain* holds? Why dost thou grudge,
Repine, and seek Removals? Be this known,

Say, who be dat which fit so easy?
O! 'tis the Man that fain would please ye;
Whom fare none but Maudgan teaze-e.
      Paw, paw, paw, &c.

Not Politician I, yet know-e
Accounts of former Times me shew-e
Dissent's a Shrub in *Britain* grow-e.
      Paw, paw, paw, &c.

That Royal Bounties flow but were they list.
Nor suit but approv'd Channels. Art thou wise?
Make it appear, establish Unity.
This, and no other Way, may'st thou cause Fame
To found to After-Ages — Lo, the Man!

And under that specious Pretence-e,
Liberty, — Uproars have commence-e,
And Freedom drove has been far hence-e.
      Paw, paw, paw, &c.

Think, think, O think! and say what mean-e,
One K— fore'd out, another lugg'd in-e;
And would you that turn out agin-e?
Or worse than that? Paw, paw, paw, &c.

Unite for Shame, and in one Common Cause
Protect our Trafic, and maintain our Laws;
So shall the jarring World, amaz'd, in Extacy
Cry out, We dare not strike! there's Unanimity!

              C. P. G.

Sold by John King *in the* Poultry, John Tinney *at the* Golden Lion *in* Fleet-Street, *and at the* Print *and* Pamphlet *Shops.*

89.   BMC 2465   May 1741   M. Ramano
An engraving of Vauxhall Gardens, much in vogue in the early 1740s. Walpole, or 'Sir Bobbee' as the accompanying verse describes him, is worked into this otherwise innocent social satire. He stands with his garter sash in the foreground, advising a fashionable young peer to abscond.

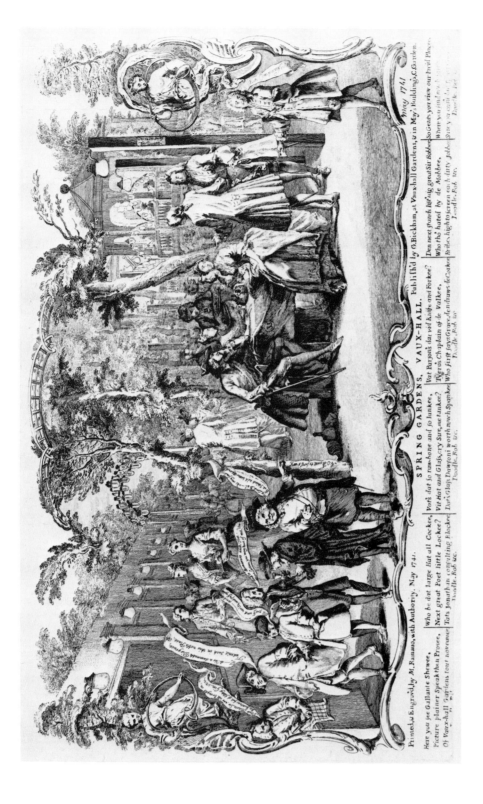

Printed & Engrav'd by M. Rumano, with Authority. May 1741.

SPRING GARDENS, VAUX-HALL. Publish'd by G. Bickham, at Vauxhall Gardens, & in May's Buildings, C. Garden.

Here you see Gallant Shewe,
Picture plainer Speak th.u Prose,
Of Vaux-hall Gardens tout hovenue
Toodle. Bob. &c.

Who be dat large Hat all Cocker,
Next great Poet little Locke?
Tats Jonathan conjuring Flocker
Toodle. Bob &c.

Vors dat so ram-bone and so lankee,
Vit hat and Glafs, cry Sure, me tankee?
Dat's Glafs Dawyoni worth much Spankee
Toodle. Bob &c.

Vat Parfons dat vid knife and Forkee?
Pyros Chaplain of de Valkee,
Who first fays Grace, de ndraws de Corkee
Toodle. Bob &c.

Den next fund lofting greatSir Bober,
Who tho hated by de Mobbee,
Brifes, high to green each fturdy Jobbee
Toodle. Bob &c.

Soo Gents, you view our brail Phizes,
Where you inf.trutt. h...
Sary u cann h. ...
Toodle. Bob. ...

May 1741

90. BMC 2498 [1741]

A comment on the general election. The semi-conscious electorate is bullied and bribed into voting for Walpole and is about to fall over the precipice into despotism. In the event the election, which further reduced an already narrow ministerial majority, proved the prelude to Walpole's fall.

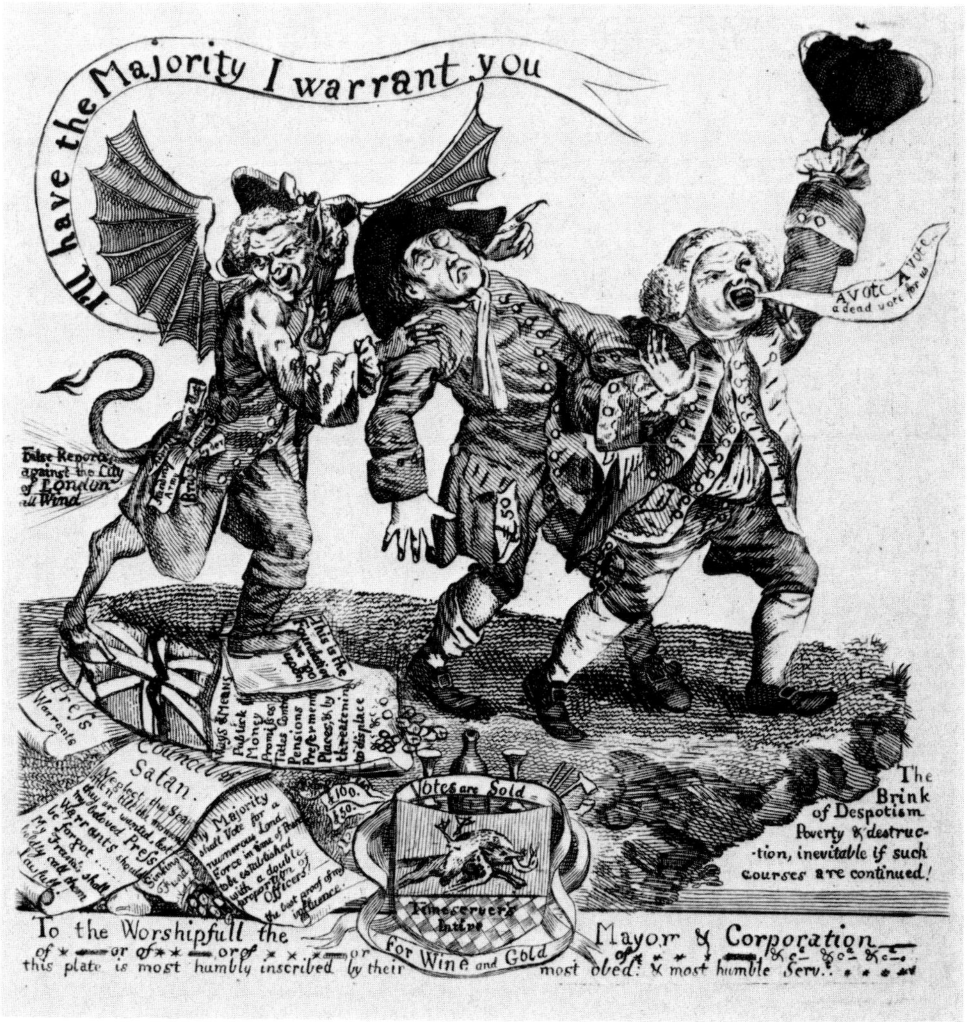
I'll have the Majority I warrant you
A Vote A Vote
a dead vote for us
False Reports against the City of London all Wind
Press Warrants
Councils of Satan.
Votes are Sold
for Wine and Gold
The Brink of Despotism
Poverty & destruction, inevitable if such courses are continued!
To the Worshipfull the Mayor & Corporation
this plate is most humbly inscribed by their most obed.t & most humble Serv.t

91. BMC 2497   2 May 1741   George Bickham

The contested election for Westminster, a large, open constituency in which popular elements were strongly represented, was much the most notable in the general election of 1741. Admiral Vernon, the victor of Portobello, and Charles Edwin, an almost unknown but wealthy Welshman, were set up against Sir Charles Wager, the First Lord of the Admiralty, and Lord Sundon, a Lord of the Treasury whose wife had been a close confidante of Queen Caroline. In a violent election contest there was much popular support for Vernon and Edwin.

To the brave Admiral Vernon, and his worthy Colleagues,
Charles Edwin, Efq; This Plate is moft humbly dedicated
By G. Bickham.

To the Independant and Worthy Electors of the Ancient City of Weftminfter: May 2 1741

O, put it in the public Voice
To make a free and worthy Choice;
Excluding fuch as would in shame
The Common wealth. Let whom we name,

Have Wifdom, Forefight, Fortitude,
Be more with Faith then Place endu'd
Whatever great One it offend:
And from the embraced Truth not bend,

Thefe neither practis'd Force, nor Forms,
Nor did they leave the Helm in Storms:
Thefe Men were truly Magiftrates;
And fuch they are make happy States.

Covent Garden Church.

92. BMC 2499   [May 1741]

The outcome of the Westminster election. Sundon prevailed on the returning officer to close the poll while he and Wager led. The result was a storm of protest and a decision by their opponents to petition the Commons against the return. In the meantime the opposition mourns its temporary defeat. The coffin of independence is borne by folly, contradiction and deceit, with the Westminster electors as mourners. The corrupt reasons for the defeat are indicated by a Jew and a bishop who discuss the bribery involved in the election, and a coalmeter who has plainly obtained his post as a reward for his vote. In the background a messenger posts for Ipswich where Vernon was actually elected (he was put up for six boroughs in all).

The funerall of Independency

Thou art at Plow on the Bank?

ParkinParnchtoba 3

Master we are all well

Thaa rat my Turn is verevell" S.F

we are all my Friends

it was ill tim:)

Bretfuren you

Smut Dode

Sam Duffy?

Auctioner   Vintner

a Barber

Kay. 174.

1 Independency Supported by Ignorance folly Contradiction & Deceit 2 The Christian Electors mourners 3 post for Vernon

93. BMC 2424   13 August 1741

A summary of Vernon's life and naval career. In the first scene Walpole says 'If he's in earnest I'm undone'. The final battle portrayed, the assault by armed forces on Cartagena, is here shown as the last of a series of brilliant successes. In fact it was a humiliating defeat, brought about by disagreements between the land and sea officers. But the opposition, anxious to collect the political reward of Vernon's enormous popularity, could not afford to admit a blemish on their hero's record.

THE ENGLISH LION *LET LOOSE,* OR *VERNON TRIUMPHANT;*

Representing in Several Scenes, the Progress of that Brave, Valiant, & Honest Admiral: *From the time of his receiving his Commission from his* MAJESTY: *to his entire Demolition of the (once thought) Impregnable Forts, defending y.e Harb.r of* Carthagena, *& his destroying the Spanish Fleet, Galleons &c.*

Publish.d according to Act of Parliament August the 15.th 1741. Price 6 pence.

94. BMC 2423   [1741]   George Bickham
     The war-news updated to 1741. On the left are shown Vernon's victory at
     Portobello and his successful, if short-lived, landing at Havana. On the right
     the failure of combined naval and military forces to take Cartagena is
     displayed above the alleged reason for this disaster: Walpole shits on a map
     of England while collecting bribes from aspiring M.P.s and placemen. The
     frame reveals that the plate for *BMC 2335* has been reworked for this print.

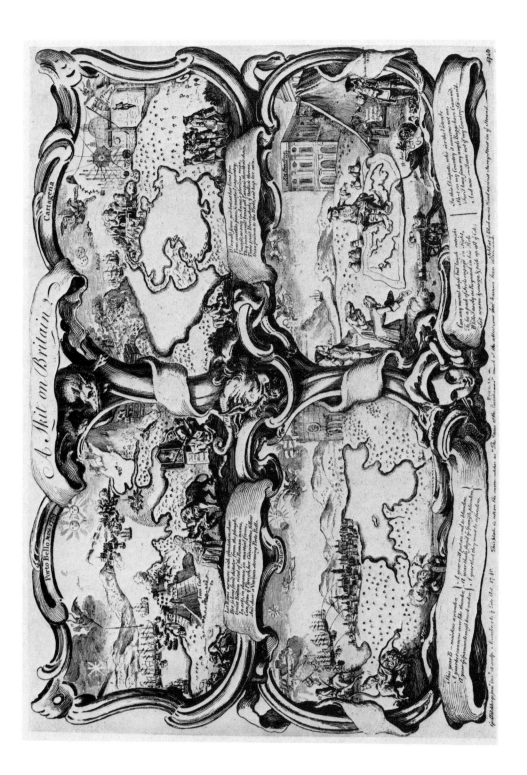

A Shit on Britain

Porto Bello   Cartagena

1740

95. BMC 2493   1741   Remigius Parr

The failure before Cartagena analysed. The army, always less popular with the press than the navy, is shown fleeing to the safety of the fleet. General Wentworth, whose dislike of Vernon was held responsible for the lack of coordination between the land and sea forces, is in one of the retreating landing craft, declaring 'I have staid as long as I care for'. The caption places ultimate responsibility with 'fatal Bob, not Fate'.

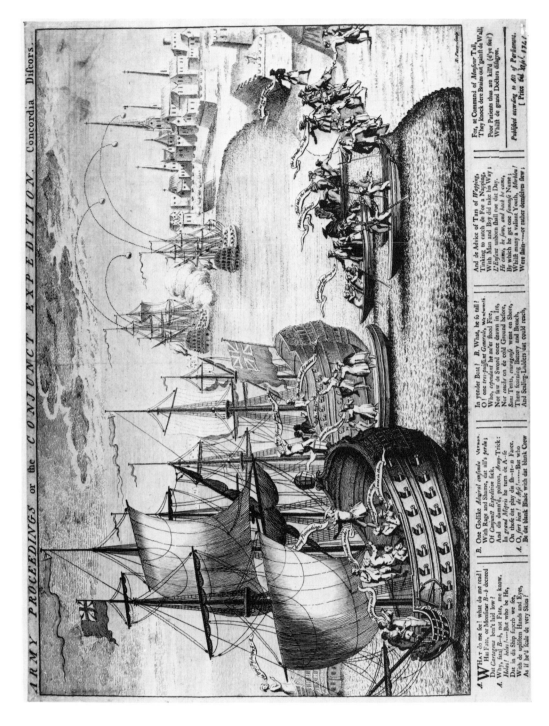

ARMY PROCEEDINGS or the CONJUNCT EXPEDITION. Concordia Difcors.

96. BMC 2464   [1741]   E. Cotin (Gerard Scotin?)
A complicated and brutal parody of the Athanasian Creed. The hieroglyph testifies (line 4) to belief in '1 [Body] of the Mon[ark], another of the prime [Minister], and another of the [Cunt]ess of Yar[mouth] . . . (line 6) The Mon[ark] corrupted, the [Minister] corrupted, and the [Cunt]ess corrupted. And yet they are [knot] only 3 Corrupted [Butt] 1 [Body] corporate corrupted'. The cartoon displays left, the trinity selling British interests abroad, and right, the scene in Cuba where Vernon's attempt to seize the island from Spain was supposed to have been defeated by Walpole's treachery and incompetence.

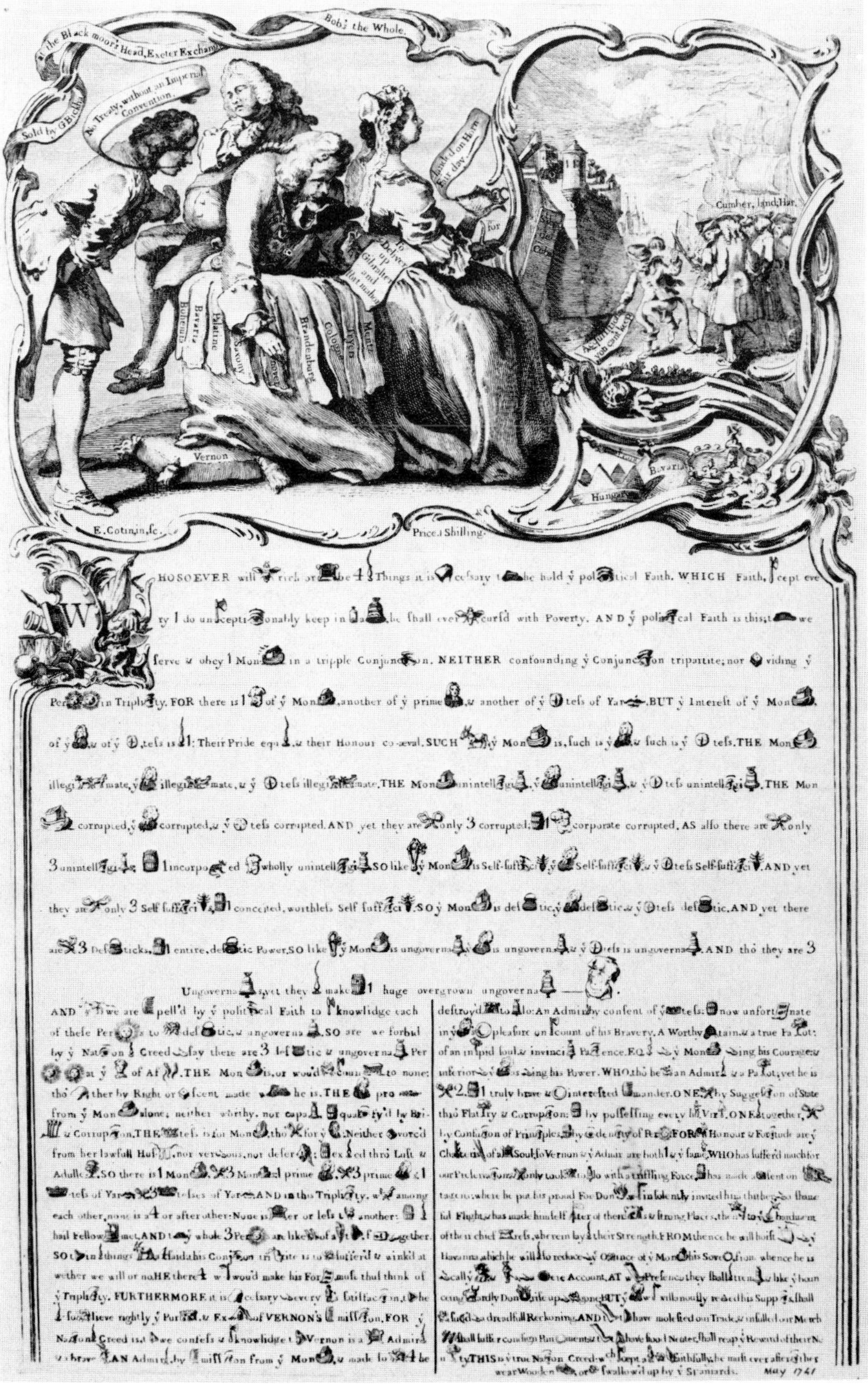
At the Black moor's Head, Exeter Exchange
Bob; the Whole.
Sold by G. Bickham
No Treaty, without an Imperial Convention.
Bavaria
Bohemia
Palatine
Saxony
Brandenburg
Cologn
Tryer
Mentz
Vernon
Cumber, land, Har.
Bavaria
Hungary

E. Cotinin, sc. Price 1 Shilling.

W HOSOEVER will rich or be 4 Things it is cefsary t he hold y pol tical Faith. WHICH Faith, cept every 1 do uncepti onably keep in a , he shall ever curs'd with Poverty. AND y political Faith is this; t we serve & obey 1 Mon in a tripple Conjunc on. NEITHER confounding y Conjunc on tripartite; nor viding y Per in Triplic ty. FOR there is 1 of y Mon , another of y prime & another of y tefs of Yar . BUT y Interest of y Mon of y & of y tefs is 1: Their Pride equ & their Honour co-æval. SUCH y Mon is, such is y & such is y tefs. THE Mon illegi mate, y illegi mate, & y tefs illegi mate. THE Mon unintell gi , y unintell gi & y tefs unintell gi . THE Mon corrupted, y corrupted, & y tefs corrupted. AND yet they are only 3 corrupted; 1 corporate corrupted. AS also there are only 3 unintell gi ; 1 incorpo ed wholly unintell gi . SO like y Mon is Self-suffi ci , y Self-suffi ci & y tefs Self-suffi ci . AND yet they are only 3 Self suffi ci s, 1 conceited, worthlefs Self suffi ci . SO y Mon is def tic, y def tic & y tefs def tic. AND yet there are 3 Def ticks, 1 entire, def tic Power. SO like y Mon is ungoverna y is ungoverna & y tefs is ungoverna . AND tho they are 3 Ungoverna s, yet they make 1 huge overgrown ungoverna —— .

AND we are pell'd by y political Faith to knowlidge each of these Per s to def tic, & ungoverna . SO are we forbid by y Nat on Creed say there are 3 def tic & ungoverna Per at y of A . THE Mon is, or would coun to none; tho ther by Right or scent made he is. THE pro from y Mon alone; neither worthy, nor capa . qual ty'd by Bri & Corrup on. THE tefs is for Mon tho for y . Neither vorc'd from her lawfull Hus , nor vert ous, nor defer ; ex ed thro Lust & Adulte . SO there is 1 Mon , 3 Mon prime , 3 prime & 1 tefs of Yar 3 tefses of Yar . AND in this Triplic ty, w among each other, none is a 4 or after other: None is er or less t another: hail Fellow met. AND t y whole 3 Per s are like of a t . SO t in things this Conj on tri ite is to suffer'd & winkt at wether we will or no. HE there w would make his For must thus think of y Triplic ty. FURTHERMORE it is cefsary every s faitfac n, t he so lieve rightly y Pur & Ex of VERNON'S miss on. FOR y Nat on Creed is, t we confess & knowlidge t Vernon is a Admir & brave AN Admir by miss on from y Mon & made so 4 he destroy'd to lo: An Admi by consent of y tefs: now unfort nate in y s pleasure on count of his Bravery. A Worthy tain, & a true Pa ot: of an insipid soul & invinci Pa ence. EQ y Mon ing his Courage, & inferior y s ing his Power. WHO tho he an Admir & a Pa ot; yet he is 2. 1 truly brave & disinterested mander. ONE by Sugges on of State thro Flat ry & Corrup on: by possessing every Vir . ONE altogether, by Confus on of Principles, by y of Per . FOR Honour & Fortitude are y Chara of a Soul, so Vernon & y Admir are both 1 & y same. WHO has suffer'd much for our Pretensions, only took to lo with a trifling Force, has made a scent on tagena; where he put his proud Foe Don who insolently invited him thither, to shameful Flight, & has made himself ter of their s & strong Places, the to hands of their chief tefs, wherein lay their Strength. FROM thence he will hoist y Havanna, which he will so reduce y Obedience of y Mon his Sove ; from whence he is y   re Account. AT Presence they shall tremble like y ceing Don up . BUT y villanously his Supp shall a dreadfull Reckoning. AND have molested our Trade & insulted our Merch shall suffer condign Punishment & they have stood Neuter, shall reap y Reward of their N ty. THIS is y true Nat on Creed, w ch cept a faithfully, he must ever after wear Wooden or swallow'd up by y Spaniards. May 1741

97.	BMC 2513	1742	Indiana

The war situation in early 1742. Maria Theresa is stripped by Frederick II of Prussia and Fleury of France. Spain creeps away with Austria's Italian provinces. George II sits back and reflects on his highly controversial convention with France, which was intended to protect Hanover. Walpole, who had declined to support Austria in the War of the Polish Succession and was supposed to have little enthusiasm for doing so in the War of the Austrian Succession, curses the Habsburg family. A number of similar prints were produced and public sympathy for Maria Theresa's plight was said to be a significant force in the formulation of British foreign policy at this time.

The Queen of Hungary Script

1742.   Indiana fct.

98. BMC 2531   1742   D. Paulicino

The fall of Walpole. In the first weeks of the new Parliament Walpole suffered a series of defeats on election petitions and related issues. The most important of these concerned the election of an opposition leader, George Lee, as Chairman of the Committee of Elections and Privileges, and the contested elections for Westminster and Chippenham. After the last of these defeats on 2 February 1742, Walpole decided to resign and take a peerage. The cartoon has him vomiting up Lee, Westminster and Chippenham. The opposition scrabbles for the offices which he has already disgorged while George II stands ready with the Earldom of Orford.

THE POLITICAL VOMIT FOR THE EASE OF BRITAIN.

He hath Swallowed down Riches and he shall Vomit them up again : GOD shall cast them out of his Belly Job XX. 15.

99. BMC 2533 1742 Designed Indiano and engraved Londini?
A variation on the purging theme. Walpole's intimates, as the opposition press
would have it, assist him in his agony. Cardinal Fleury administers a clyster
from the rear, and Walpole's illegitimate daughter, Lady Churchill, attends to
his private parts. A vision of Walpole and the devil driving for France appears
above.

Bro. Robert
under his Last
Purgation

100. BMC 2536   [February–March 1742]
Walpole goes to the Lords. The scene is the Court of Requests, the lobby between the two chambers. Justice expels Walpole from the Commons while Pulteney and his friends look on. Walpole is welcomed by the peers. He clutches his head and says: 'I go in hope to save this, and trust to the hat'. He stood in real danger of impeachment and depended on his new status and on the king to avert it.

FROM ONE HOUSE TO AN OTHER.

Triumphant V——y too will succeed;   But Justice, tho' she's tardy, will prevail,
When Power, Lion-like, to Honour leads.   And holds the Sword pois'd equal with the Scale;
The Supplicant Crew of C——t may approve,   The Country claims its Due.— Protectors vain,
And join to usher in the Grand Remove.   And this H——se will wipe out the Others Stain.

Publish'd according to Act of Par[l].t Feb.18.1742.

Price 6.pence.
№ 516. 1742.

101. BMC 2537   [March 1742]
The wheel of fortune finally turns against Walpole and his supporters, while his enemies ascend with it. Not all the latter can be identified, but Argyll leads the ascent of the wheel, followed by Pulteney, a Tory who is given assistance by a Jacobite, and Sandys, who now loses interest in the place bill with which his name has been associated.

THE WHEEL OF FORTUNE, OR, THE SCOT'S STEP, COMPLETED.

102. BMC 2451   [1742]

A comment on the split which occurred within the opposition on Walpole's fall. Pulteney and Carteret joined the ministry while Argyll led the Tories in unsuccessful demands for a broad-based coalition. Here George II (identified by his kicking foot) plays with Sir Robert who is given the credit for striking Argyll (the shuttlecock) out of court. The Prince of Wales, though he owed his reconciliation with his father to Argyll, rejoices. The opportunity is taken for some obscene comments on George II. Lady Yarmouth, his mistress, complains 'Your Cockee my Love mounts rarely in Yarmouth' and Walpole's illegitimate daughter, Lady Churchill, declares her readiness to replace her in the king's affections: 'Dad I'm a match for your Partner'.

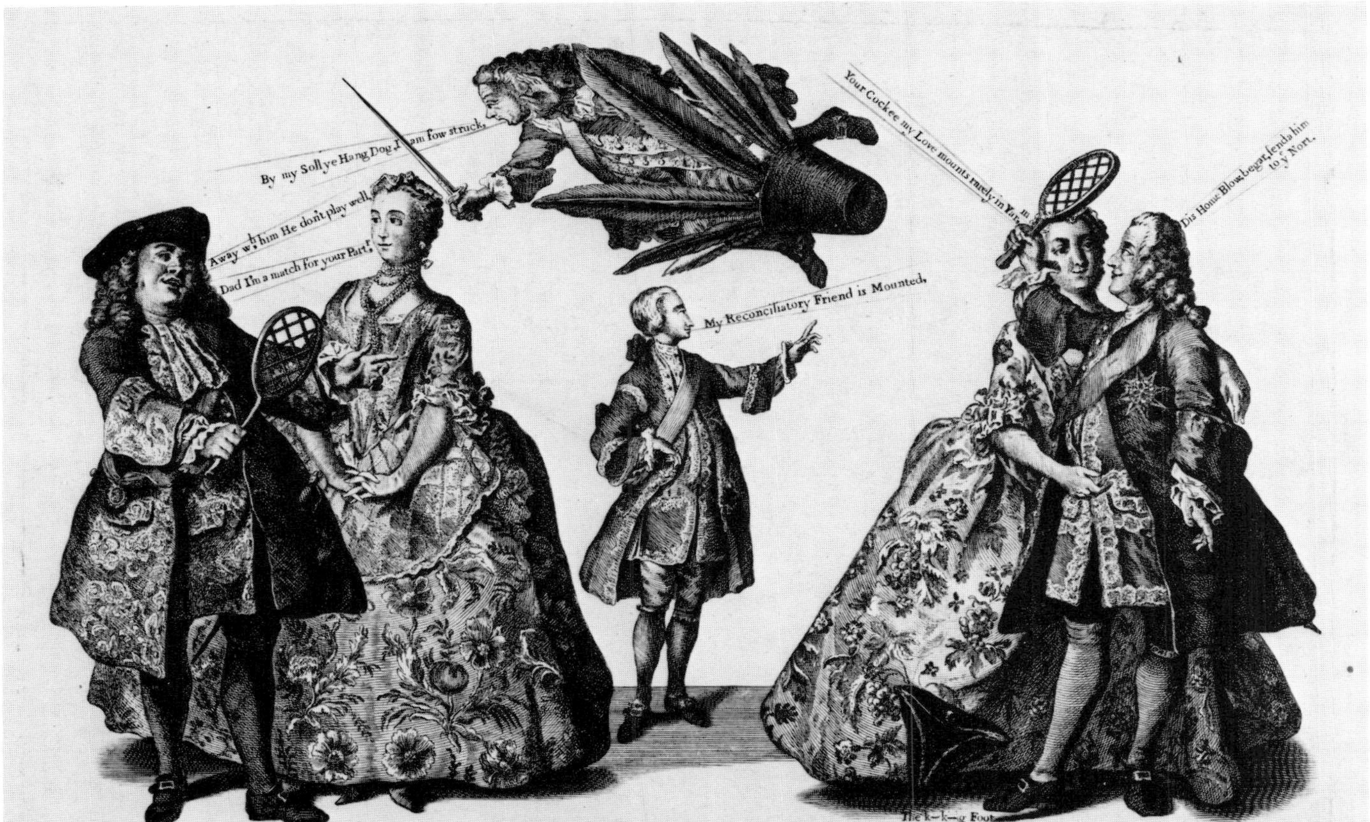
By my Soll ye Hang Dog I am fow struck,
Away wt him He don't play well,
Dad I'm a match for your Part.
My Reconcilistory Friend is Mounted,
Your Cockee my Love mounts rarely in
Dis House Blowbegot, send a him to y Nort.
The k—k—g Foot

THE C——T SHITTLE-COCK.

103. BMC 2538   [March 1742]
Disillusionment follows victory. Pulteney's decision to accept a peerage caused a wave of revulsion against him. Here he removes the mask of the patriot and reveals his true face.

THE TREACHEROUS PATRIOT UNMASK'D

A Man may be known

by his look. Eccles: 19. 29.

This is the Mask he wore 'till the memorable 11th. of March.

You are all Bit, Ha ha ha!

price 6.d

Unmask'd, with bare-fac'd Insolence and Sneer,
Behold your Patriot — who from year t' year
Flatter'd your hopes with promis'd relief;
Now laughs with Scorn at your too fond belief!
The face he wore e're he beguild your trust,
Bespoke an honest heart, upright and just:

But wonder not; since thus you see his face,
That he's ungrateful, Treacherous and Base.
Let Loyal minds with patience drag their Chain,
Despise his Smiles; his Frowns with scorn disdain;
This Sneering St—tes—n may be cloath'd with shame,
When fetter'd Loyliste shall be Crown'd with fame.

* We know not of your Majesties having among us an open, a secret or suspected enemy. Dissenters addrys.

104. BMC 2540 18 March 1742
Further disillusionment. It had been widely anticipated that Walpole would be prosecuted for his alleged crimes. But neither the new ministry nor the committee appointed to consider his case showed much interest in such action, and it was plausibly assumed that Walpole's resignation had resulted from a deal guaranteeing his safety. The print revives the old device of the screen, in this case screening Walpole himself. At the top the king and the Prince of Wales are reconciled, and the end of the Whig opposition signalised. The screen itself displays Walpole's crimes; a mirror reveals Walpole himself standing behind it, working the strings which control M.P.s in the Commons below. Argyll, who sought a genuine coalition of Whigs and Tories and was consequently the patriot hero of the hour, points the moral.

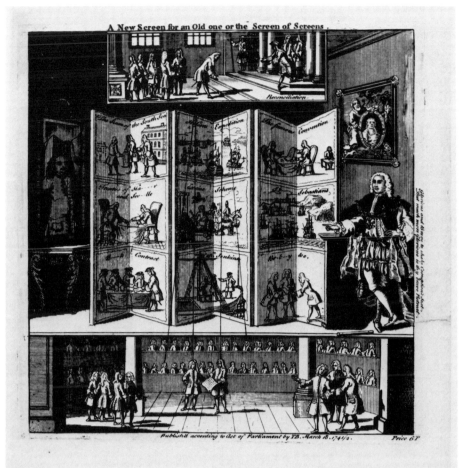

A New Screen for an Old one or the Screen of Screens.

Published according to Act of Parliament by T.B. March 18. 1741/2.

Price 6d.

The SCREEN. *A* SIMILE.

DEAR *William*, did'st thou never go
To mimic Farce, call'd *Puppet-Shew?*
There, *William*, did'st thou never see
Of Figures great Variety?
With a big Belly comes a Fellow,
In blustering Mood, call'd *Punchinello*;
He roars and swaggers, bounces, swears,
Giving himself a thousand Airs;
Knocks Puppets down, and makes a Boast,
That he alone will rule the Roast.

   But when *Punch* is turn'd off the Stage,
Some other Puppets come t'engage:
With other Motions, other Faces,
Act some new Part, to shew their Graces.

Alas! dear *William*, all this while,
A Trickster does your Sense beguile:
Behind that SCREEN there stands a Wight, *walpole*
Safely conceal'd from publick Sight:
He was the *Punch* at first you saw;
He gives the other Puppets Law;
And by his secret Strings he still
Governs the others as he will;
And all the Difference that is known,
You only hear *another Tone:*
The *Puppet Man,*——behind the *Screen,*
Is the same Man,——although not seen.

   Lond. Evening Post, Mar. 11, 1741-2.

105. BMC 2559   12 April 1742

A variant on the theme of the screen. Exhibited are Walpole's crimes, beginning with the corruption in his office of Treasurer of the Navy for which he had been expelled from Parliament in 1712, and ending with his anticipated trial and the block. In front of the screen Walpole advises the king to divide the new ministers by means of bribery. To the left of the screen Argyll declares his intention to resign.

The NIGHT-VISIT, or the RELAPSE:

With the PRANKS of BOB FOX the JUGLER, while STEWARD to Lady BRIT. display'd on a SCREEN.

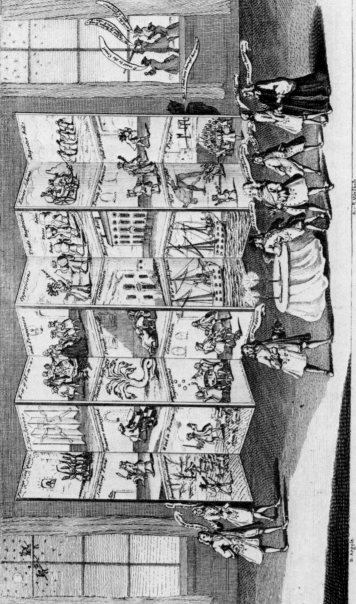

D. Argyle.

4.—R. Walpole.

Explanation of the SCREEN.

1. He is sent to Goal for selling Oats and Hay out of his Lady's Stables.—Getting at Liberty again, he transforms himself into a Screen, to protect a Gang of Thieves who had robbed the House, and with whom he went Snacks.

2. Having introduced a common Strumpet, called *Corruption*, into the Family, and bribed over the major Part of the Lady's Servants by Presents and enlarging their Wages, he first trick'd her out of a large Settlement, in favour of her chief Son, beyond what Law or Money could afford; and then take out a Statute of Lunacy against her, vesting in her said Servants as Trustees, all the Issues and Profits of her Estate, to be disposed of as Himself should think fit.

3. Instead of clearing off the Incumbrances which clogged the Estate, he runs it more in Debt. He next studies how to vex the Tenants; forces them to take new Leases at Rack-Rent, and payexorbitant Fines and Dues: Also to maintain a great Number of Bailiffs and Runners, which he kept for collecting the same; and perpetually harrassed them, by taking out Ejectments, or subduing them for Trespasses.

4. He grew so audacious as to propose that the Chariot of his Lady's Son should be drawn by the Tenants instead of Horses, while he sat in the Coach-Box to flog them on.—The Trustees would have consented; but he durst not venture to proceed when it came to the Pub, for fear of a Knock that first Time he appeared abroad.

5. He murdered his own Child, whom he pretended a more than ordinary Fondness for, in order to get the Disposal of the Effects which had been left him by an Uncle.—Next He robs his Lady of sufficient Money, which never were made; for Necessaries of the House and Stock for the Land, which never were sent in; and cheats her of more, by bringing in Bills, for Repairs for Expences in Law-suits, which never were carried on: Always adding a swinging Article, for Services which he never made known to her.

6. His iniquitous Conduct being highly refented by his Lady, he conjures up a horrible Monster, in Form of a *Hydra*, to awe and terrify her.—After this, he turns Papist, and takes a *French* Jesuit for his Confessor, to whom he discovered all the Secrets of his Lady's Family.

7. He lets the Mansion-House, then much decayed, run to Ruin for want of Repair; pulls down some of

the main Beams that supported it, with great Part of the Foundation Wall; takes away the Partitions of the middle Floor, and throws the whole into one.—At the same time he builds a splendid House like a Palace for himself, with Part of the Spoils of his Lady's.

8. He holds the Hands of an *Austrian* Nobleman, who was his Lady's intimate Friend, while a *Frenchman* buffets him, and a *Spaniard* runs away with his Hat and Wig.

9. Being bribed by Don *Faithboy* and M. *Dupont*, two of her Neighbours, he suffers the first to cut down the Woods about her, and the latter to steal the black Castle off the Lands, and the latter to fleal the Sheep for many Years together, without suffering the Tenants to hinder them, or make Reprisals.

10. At a Meeting with Monfieur and the Don, for accommodating Matters amicably, he gives up all the Tenants Demands for Damages, upon the Don's bare Promise in Writing not to injure them for the future. The Breach of this Agreement brings on a second Accommodation; the second a third, and so on, much move to the Advantage of the Steward than a Law-suit would have been, which therefore he was always against.—In the List of their Meetings, he releafed a Debt of 250 l.

due on Ballance to the Tenants, in lieu of the Don's Note for only 17 l. payable fix Months after, which *Bil Fax* called Prompt-Payment.

11. The Tenants hereupon clamouring more loudly than ever, to appeafe them he commenced a Suit against the Don: but after putting his Lady to fix times the Expence necessary to prepare for Trial, he suffers her to be non-suited, for want partly of sending the Witnefies, and partly of giving proper Instructions to her Council in their Briefs.

12. His fraudulent and treacherous Dealing becoming now fo flagrant, that fome even of his Cronies began to defert his Interest, he takes to his Heels, and endeavours to escape from his Purfuers, by throwing Gold Dust in their Eyes, and other Artifices.—Being taken and tried for several of the aforementioned Crimes he was condemned, and, pursuant to Sentence, received the Punishment due to his Demerits.

Published April 12, 1742, *by* J. Huggonfon, *in* Sweetings Rents, *near* Bucklet-Court *in* League Hill.

Ap. 1742

106.   BMC 2543   24 April 1742

Walpole protects himself from prosecution. The committee set up by the House of Commons to investigate Walpole's corrupt practices, could get nothing out of Nicholas Paxton, one of the key witnesses as Walpole's Treasury Solicitor. Paxton refused to give evidence on the grounds that he might incriminate himself and was accordingly committed to Newgate. Here he languishes in his cell while his companion warns him that he will meet the same fate as those involved in the Atterbury Plot in 1722. The gaoler prevents the bringing of pen and ink while Walpole peers through the window. The pictures show one of the corrupt parliamentary elections at which Paxton was alleged to have connived and Walpole padlocking Paxton's mouth.

The Solicitor COMMITTED, or the Dumb Screen.

 Opprsion'd Tool.! well qualif'yd, no lobe;   Nicholas Paxton; Sister to the   But sure his   Quirks Shame ye CORRUPTOR screen.
To Bribe a Borough; Cham insult y Prefs; }Fixing on his Prospects by the}   His Masters Guilt is in his Silence seen. 24. Ap. 1742.
                                            Publish'd according to Act of Parliament Apr. 24. 1742.   Price 6 pence.

107. BMC 2551 [July 1742]
Walpole saved from retribution. Attempts to prosecute him quickly petered out and in July 1742 Parliament was prorogued. George II (left) and Walpole (right) are here shown bidding defiance to Britannia and Justice respectively. Above, a mask and a fox, below, a public execution. On the left ships are waiting to carry the king off to Hanover; on the right the gallows await Walpole.

Touch me not; OR B⚓b's Defiance.

Behold two Patriots of our British Land
Join'd Head to Head, instead of Hand to Hand!
When two such Noddles are laid close together,
What Tempests in y̌ State can Shatter Either?—
                                                  Geo. II

I and the K—g, the haughty W—l—ev cry'd,
And All y̌ Malice of his Foes defy'd;
But R—n, haughtier still, (t'evade Disaster)
Cries, Touch me not if you can,— and not my Master.
 Sir Rob. Walpole.   Endeavty into conduct of Sr R. W.— Bolinbrollé. Bk. n. OK. vii. Sec. 22.

Ap. 1742.

108. BMC 2575   [August 1742]
A sardonic comment on the sequel to Walpole's fall. A raree-show displays the tricks and dispenses the bounty of politics to rapturous patriot politicians. A new opposition is already being led into action by a two-faced master of ceremonies. At a window a nurse shows a child with the words 'Dad's own face' – i.e. the new ministry of Carteret and Pulteney is indistinguishable from Walpole's. At the next window George II farts on the throng below; he wipes his posterior with the latest report of the Commons committee set up to investigate Walpole's crimes.

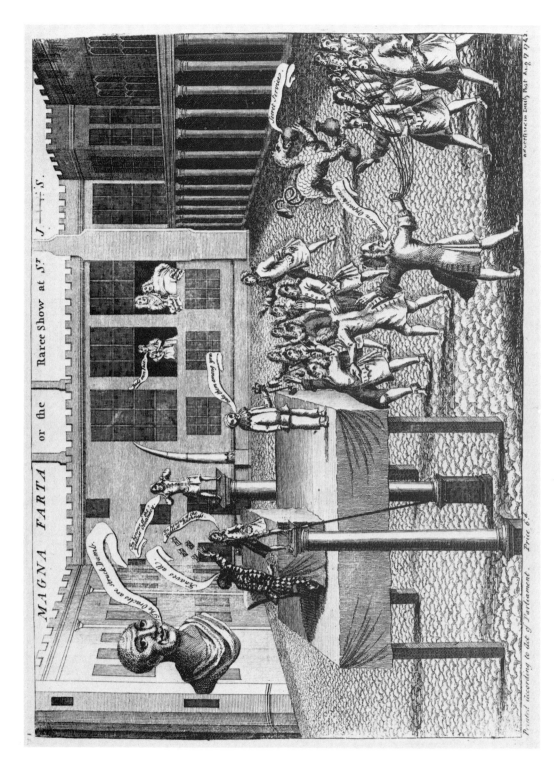

MAGNA FARTA or the Raree Show at S.T J———'S.

Printed according to Act of Parliament. Price 6d.

109. BMC 2607   3 December 1743   George Bickham
A retrospective judgement on the nature of Walpole's rule, based on the 1743
edition of Pope's *Dunciad*, which was more explicit as to politics than the
original edition.

THE late P—m—r M—n—r.

1743 Dec.ʳ 3

Lo! What are all your Schemes come to?

Publish'd by G. Bickham in May's Buildings

More he had faid, but yawn'd——All Nature nods:
What Mortal can refift the Yawn of Gods?
Churches and Chapels inftantly it reach'd,
St. James's firft, for leaden G—ll—t preach'd;
Then catch'd the Schools; the Hall fcarce kept awake;
The Convocation gap'd, but could not fpeak.
Loft was the Nation's Senfe, nor could be found,

While the long folemn Unifon went round;
Wide, and more wide, it fpread o'er all the realm;
Ev'n Palinurus nodded at the Helm;
The Vapour mild o'er each Committee crept;
Unfinifh'd Treaties in each Office flept;
And Chief-lefs Armies doz'd out the Campaign;
And Navies yawn'd for Orders on the Main.

DUNCIAD.

110. BMC 2629   [1745]

The death of Walpole. He is seen off to hell by the doctor whom he had consulted in his last, painful illness, by Pelham, his eventual successor as prime minister, and by Sir John Hynde Cotton, leader of the broad-bottom Tories who had now joined the government. On the left Carteret and Bath, once again out of office, are handing over their mail for the next world. All those depicted, the caption explains, are 'Pluto's Ministers'.

Courier just Setting out. (Who has any Letters to Send,) Dispatches from y^e Life which his Broken pen gr...

A Mail for Plute.

At length Old O——d must depart.
Help'd on by medicinal Art:
B——h, Gr——le, P——m, C——n Sends, (for whose'er on Earth they join
Lick his one Duty, and his Friends: All Plute's Minifters are dam'n.

C. Yr Majefty may depend on me. B. And on me. M. Difpatch.   P. I'll promote his Intereft.   The Broad Bottoms are his Friends.

16 March. 1757.

111. [c.1730s] J. Cooper
A formal portrait of Walpole. A comparison of this with the work of the satirists of the time suggests that they achieved their effects more by the use of mechanical devices and symbols than by the representation or caricature of facial features.

The Right Honble Sr Robert Walpole,

First Lord Commissioner of the Treasury, Chancellor of the Exchequer, Knight of the most Noble
Order of the Garter, and one of His Majestys most Honble Privy Council.

J. Cooper Excudit.

FURTHER READING

The most recent biography is H. T. Dickinson, *Walpole and the Whig Supremacy* (1973). A more extensive but as yet incomplete account is to be found in J. H. Plumb, *Sir Robert Walpole* (1956, 1960). William Coxe's *Memoirs of the Life and Administration of Sir Robert Walpole* (3 vols., 1798) remains an invaluable source of detailed information. A useful collection of essays on the Walpole era is J. Black, ed. *Britain in the Age of Walpole* (1984); among monographs bearing on particular aspects of Walpole's career, are J. M. Beattie, *The English Court in the reign of George I* (1967); J. Carswell, *The South Sea Bubble* (1961); P. G. M. Dickson, *The Financial Revolution in England* (1967); P. Fritz, *The English Ministers and Jacobitism, 1715–1745* (1975); E. Hughes, *Studies in Administration and Finance* (1934); P. Langford, *The Excise Crisis – Society and Politics in the Age of Walpole* (1975); J. B. Owen, *The Rise of the Pelhams* (1957); J. H. Plumb, *The Growth of Political Stability in England, 1675–1725* (1967); C. B. Realey, *The Early Opposition to Sir Robert Walpole, 1720–1727* (1931); L. Colley, *In Defiance of Oligarchy: The Tory Party 1714–60* (1982).

The more approachable primary sources in print are R. Sedgwick, *Some Materials Towards Memoirs of the Reign of King George II, by John, Lord Hervey* (3 vols., 1931), and Historical Manuscripts Commission, *Egmont Diary* (3 vols.).

Particularly important for the cartoons of the Walpole era are the intellectual and literary aspects of politics. These may be studied in H. T. Dickinson, *Bolingbroke* (1970); I. Kramnick, *Bolingbroke and His Circle* (1968); J. Loftis, *The Politics of Augustan Drama* (1963); M. Mack, *The Garden and the City* (1969); R. Paulson, *Emblem and Expression: Meaning in English Art of the Eighteenth Century* (1975); B. A. Goldgar, *Walpole and the Wits: The Relation of Politics to Literature, 1722–1742* (1976); W. A Speck, *Society and Literature in England 1700–60* (1983); F. P. Lock, *The Politics of Gulliver's Travels* (1980) and *Swift's Tory Politics* (1983); M. Percival, ed.; *Political Ballads Illustrating the Administration of Sir Robert Walpole* (1916).

On the cartoons themselves the outstanding authorities are M. D. George, *English Political Caricature to 1792. A Study of Opinion and Propaganda* (1959) and H. M. Atherton, *Political Prints in the Age of Hogarth: A Study of the Ideographic Representation of Politics* (1974).

Their artistic background is illuminated by many studies of Hogarth, the most important of these being R. Paulson, *Hogarth's Graphic Works* (2 vols., 1965).

Also particularly worthy of note is D. G. Kunzle, *The Early Comic Strip, c1450–1825* (1973), who traces the tradition of narrative art in prints and engravings, devoting a substantial portion of his work to the age of Hogarth.